# Travels with Odysseus: Uncommon Wisdom from Homer's *Odyssey*

Michael J. Goldberg

Circe's Island Press
Tempe, Arizona

Library of Congress Control Number: 2005902852

ISBN: 0-9767915-0-1

First published in 2006

Circe's Island Press
PO Box 11628
Tempe, AZ 85284
www.TravelswithOdysseus.com

Printed in the United States of America

The paper used in this book complies with the Permanent Paper Standard issued by the National Information Standards Organization (Z39.48-1984).

Goldberg, Michael J. 1948–
Travels with Odysseus/ Michael J. Goldberg
p. cm.

ISBN 0-9767915-0-1

Homer. Odyssey—Handbooks, manuals, etc. 2. Odysseus (Greek Mythology)
3. Enneagram

Cover design by Howard Grossman/12E Design
Interior design by Michele DeFilippo of 1106 Design

For Nancy Jean Amick, PhD

## CONTENTS

**PART FOUR:**

# PART ONE

# Introduction

*This is not a journey for the feet.*
— Plotinus

*Every journey has secret destinations*
*of which the traveler is unaware.*
— Martin Buber

*There is a Bible in every wanderer's bedroom,*
*where there might better be* The Odyssey.
— James Hillman

Homer's *Odyssey* is the great story of homecoming.

Since ancient times, *The Odyssey* has been known as the journey that each one of us — having been out and about, struggling one way or another, pretending to be this and that — must take to return Home, to who we really are and what we are supposed to become.

On his long odyssey, Odysseus gets sidetracked, distracted, waylaid. Some truths he learns easily and others he resists.

He meets magical and powerful beings, who can help the journey along or cause disaster. Some see who he is in his heart and help him, and bring him insight and attainment. Others — aggravating and difficult strangers — try to do him in.

In all of this, Odysseus is not so different than the rest of us.

Homer is at the soul of storytelling, but he was far more than a wondrous storyteller. It would be hard to overstate his vast influence.

His two epic poems, *The Iliad* and *The Odyssey,* are the first grand narratives of the Western imagination; for the nearly 140 generations since he recounted these adventures (from about 750 BCE), philosophers and warriors and tellers of tales have claimed the hero Odysseus as *one of their own,* at the ancient roots of their diverse traditions.

Homer was said to be a wanderer, which meant that his stories were not provincial, not limited by time or place. He was unlearned, so that he was not tied to the official story of the times. And he was by tradition blind, which, in the conventions of mythology, suggests that he saw what others did not.

And indeed, for ancient audiences, Homer's stories of great but flawed heroes who wrangled with fabulous monsters, sensuous witches and evil foreigners (not to mention those petulant gods and goddesses who shamelessly meddled in human affairs), percolated with profound meanings. In fact, the true focus of Homer's stories was said to be a *sacred wisdom* describing "the fate of souls and the structure of the universe."[1]

The fifth century philosopher Proclus wrote that for those who were perceptive enough to appreciate it, Homer's poems taught what he called "a secret doctrine," by which he seemed to mean not some musty theology, but more like a working perspective on life, a way of being in the world, a most *practical* way of traveling the journey Home.

A myth like *The Odyssey* plays out on several levels.

The travels of Odysseus take place in the realm of the psyche, as if in a dream. And, as in a dream, we play all the parts. We are not only Odysseus, the bedraggled traveler who becomes a hero, but also the brutish Cyclops, shrewd Circe and the rest. With each adventure, the characters of our internal drama jockey for position.

But, perhaps more startling, these stories are the stuff of what we call the outer world as well. So often, psychologically minded people look inward for meaning, when staring us right in the face is the Cyclops himself, barely disguised as the overbearing boss or street tough.

Odysseus is nothing if not a practical man, a traveler in the real world. From him we learn the nitty-gritty facts of life about the long journey Home.

## *The Iliad* and *The Odyssey*

*Was this the face that launched a thousand ships?*
*And burnt the topless towers of Ilium?*
*Sweet Helen, make me immortal with a kiss.*
— MARLOWE, *DR. FAUSTUS*

The story before our story is the bloody Trojan War, a 10 year struggle over the most beautiful woman in the world, named Helen. She was married to King Menelaus of Sparta. But Paris,

Prince of Troy (Ilium in the Greek), spirited her away (with her consent or not, we can only wonder, since versions differ).

Menelaus gathered his fellow Greek kings to fight the Trojan War for the return of his queen. *The Iliad* recounts the events in the last year of that 10 year war — it was 1184 BCE — when the Greeks finally win and Helen returns with the triumphant Menelaus to Sparta.

*The Iliad's* warriors venture out to do battle; they win conquests and recover from defeats. They build their egos and test their powers. They are generally not shy about demanding their way or asserting their will.

*The Iliad* is about devising strategy and taking action, about fighting for what you want against others who want it too; it is the story of how to (or how not to) make your place in the world.

Odysseus is the shrewdest of the Greek generals. He thought up one of the most famous and devious military stratagems of all time: to concoct a colossal, hollow wooden horse, secretly station battle-ready Greek soldiers inside, and present it as a gift to the citizens of Troy. The Trojans received the impressive gift horse into their city and, when the hidden Greek warriors snuck out at night, the stunned Trojans were caught unawares and were bushwhacked; the Greeks won the final victory. (These days, an apparently benign computer program which contains secret directives to wreak havoc is called a Trojan Horse.)

Now, the war over, Odysseus plans a swift journey home to the Greek island of Ithaca, just across the Aegean Sea from Troy (on the modern Turkish coast); it is a distance of 565 nautical miles, no more than a fortnight's sail. Alas, the trip takes Odysseus 10 years. The account of this famous, problematical sea voyage is told in *The Odyssey*, "the journey of Odysseus."

# PART TWO

CHAPTER ONE

# The Lotos Eaters
# Desire under the Helm

*O human being, why do you sleep?... Why do you not search out the house of your heart?*

— Hildegard of Bingen

*How do you expect to arrive at the end of your own journey if you take the road to another man's city? How do you expect to reach your own perfection by leading somebody else's life?*

— Merton

Soon after leaving Troy, Odysseus and his fleet make landfall at a sleepy backwater port which is the Land of the Lotos Eaters.

The Land of the Lotos Eaters straddles two worlds. Odysseus, a great war hero, is leaving the competitive, combative, outer-directed and ego-oriented realm of *The Iliad,* centered on conquests, one-upmanship and material accomplishments. This is the world that we know.

He could continue on as he has, business as usual, sacking cities and claiming treasure, expanding his reputation and influence, and getting very rich. If he did nothing more in his life, Odysseus would still be remembered as famous and successful, the shrewdest of the Greeks at Troy. He could rest on his laurels. We would still be reading about him, although perhaps not with such consequence.

Or he can change direction and head for Home; this is the difficult inner journey toward a deepening of meaning, and toward who he really is supposed to be — king and husband and father — and what he really wants.

Lotos Land is at the fork in the road. It is where the people who can't decide which way to go get stuck.

Like some coffeehouse beatniks of another era, Lotos Eaters are an easygoing, no-hassle, copacetic tribe that goes with the warm-and-fuzzy flow. They are the first counter-culture in Western literature.

But underneath their super-languid persona, they have a dark secret: they are drug addicts, hooked on an herb called lotos. And they are pushers too: they share their noxious weed with the sailors Odysseus has sent ashore.

When he hears that his men have taken lotos, Odysseus storms off his ship, furious, a one-man shore patrol. He collects his stoned, disoriented sailors. He lashes them to the ship's rowing benches (for they fight hard to stay in Lotos Land), and they urgently sail on.

Why does lotos stall the journey? Why is Odysseus so alarmed?

## Home

*The opposite of home is not distance but forgetfulness.*

— Elie Weisel

Lotos is not just some mellow herbal tea. It's a potent narcotic that triggers a specific, disastrous amnesia: everyone who takes lotos loses all memory of Home.

What's the big deal?

Home is where the heart is of course, the place where you are most *at-home* in the world; it is the place, safe "beyond the reach of the perils of wayfaring,"[2] where you are not a stranger, where your most private struggles are known and understood, and where you are seen and appreciated for your special virtues, your own unique powers. Home, at essence, is where you are *recognized* for who you really are, not more and not less. When you make yourself at home, you show your true nature, no matter where you are.

Home is not only the world that knows *you*, but it's where you can recognize the world for what it is, where you can see clearly without exaggeration or distortion, inflation or deflation. Free from pretense, you can see past appearances, past roles or titles, past your fears and projections and defenses, to glimpse someone else's true nature. Home is where you can get out of your own way.

From the perspective of the psyche, each traveler holds deep in the soul the knowledge of the place where he or she is most real, most easily seen for who one is, and where he or she need not pretend to be more or different than that. That place, of course, is your true Home.

It is unlikely to be some Great Mystery. Most travelers could tell you without much trouble what being at-home is like (or would be like) for them.

For Odysseus, Home is the small, rocky island of Ithaca where his beloved wife and soul mate Penelope awaits, and so does his real life as king and husband and father. Homer's principal epithet for Ithaca is "clear-seen:" it is the place where one sees and is seen clearly.

Until he gets there, no matter how edifying his travels, no matter how welcoming and supportive the natives, no matter how divine the goddesses along the way, Odysseus is everywhere a foreigner, a refugee from the wars. Later on, Calypso is the hostess with the mostess, and the Phaecians sing Odysseus' praises; both ask him to stay on and mean it, but he is not at-home even in their fulsome care. Each new stop means an alien nation, where he is, at least in part, not quite known or knowable.

The psychologist Carl Jung called this very sort of journey home *individuation*, the arduous journey to "divest the self of false wrappings,"[3] as he put it, so as to engage and express the true self. "Individuation," Jung wrote, "is a process by which a man becomes the definite, unique being he in fact is," so that he fulfills a particular calling which is distinctively his own.[4]

If home is the place where you are most yourself, then the distance between who you are pretending to be, your "false wrappings" as Jung has it, and who you really are, is how far you are from home. For Odysseus, it is a long and difficult trip.

For Lotos Eaters, the memory of Home is wiped out. Without the possibility to be at-Home in the world, then no matter how ingenious or fervent or fearless the traveler, he or she is utterly lost. *There's nothing to set your compass by.* Heck, there's not much reason to leave comfy Lotos Land.

That would be bad enough. But Home is not just the destination of this voyage: *Home is at the root of all wanting and choosing. All desires* are desires to get closer to Home one way or another, to be more at-Home in the world.

Lotos Eaters, for all their pleasantness, have no desires at all; they've snuffed them out with their deadening drug. Oh, they may have *preferences* during their day; they may decisively prefer

Cherry Garcia over plain vanilla. But, as they amble through life, *they are unable to heartfully choose one path of action over another* because they have fallen asleep to their guidepost, their Home: who they really are and what they are supposed to become. They are stuck at this fork in the road, unable to choose a direction.

No wonder Odysseus is so concerned.

## Lotos Eaters

What is lotos?

Some travelers forget themselves with actual drugs or alcohol, and lotos can be that; lotos can be food or sex or any of the fashionable addictions of the moment, but lotos need not be a conventional jones. It could be a television or Internet habit, a humdrum job or an inflexible daily routine. It could be that long-time relationship of convenience: you know the one, comforting in a way perhaps, but smothering and without passion.

For workaholics, lotos shows up as more work, more projects, a larger stack in the in-box. Overactivity is the lotos that keeps Type A people so stuck in their trance that they fail to remember their real Home.

We've all had times when we've forgotten ourselves and where we were headed, when we were pressed into the agendas of others, got swept along, and then later regretted it. ("Damn. What was I thinking?"). We've had a serving of lotos.

But Lotos Eaters make a life's work of forgetting their real selves. They put themselves aside, stifle their own yearnings, and periodically wake up to find themselves a supporting cast member in someone else's play. They may find themselves at midlife feeling frustrated and betrayed for having given up their own journey for reasons that no longer make sense.

They may have had their good reasons once. Perhaps they worked hard as children to keep peace in a big family or in a contentious community. For the sake of the group, they stuffed down their true feelings and inclinations, and put their own journey aside. They learned to hide behind a pleasant smile and not to rock the boat, most especially not to express opinions, but rather to be the conciliator. They sold themselves out for the sake of surface harmony, a very high price to pay.

As adults, Lotos Eaters are easygoing, laid-back, humble, and non-directive. They avoid decisions. They don't let their wants get in the way, and they are not swept up by strong yearnings. These are the genial, over-accommodating people who go along to get along, resigned to accept the life they find in front of them. Ah, well.

I have a dear colleague in Iowa; I love to go there to teach and consult. When we go to a restaurant I usually ask the server what's in the dish, and how is it prepared. My colleague is uncomfortable with this level of inquiry. "You're in Iowa now," she says, "and in Iowa we take what we are given, and we learn to like it." This is the Lotos Eater approach.

Lotos Eaters go along and accommodate. Under the guise of making themselves more comfortable and at home in the world, they are less themselves; they stifle their passions.

Danish philosopher Søren Kierkegaard wrote: "Let others complain that the age is wicked, my complaint is that it is wretched for it lacks passion... This is the reason my soul always turns back to the Old Testament and to Shakespeare. I feel that those who speak there are at least human beings; they hate, they love, they murder their enemies."[5]

Relaxed, easygoing, meditative, without apparent longing, not so hung up as the rest of us, Lotos Eaters may seem to others, and even to themselves, to be *already* home. They may appear spiritually advanced because they do not itch to be on the road as others do. Like some newly-minted meditator, they smile benignly at those who get all hot and bothered.

But being narcotized is not the same thing as being in harmony. A self-satisfied Lotos Eater may think he or she is at peace with the world, just going with the flow. But there is no flow; there is only stagnation.

This is not to say that Lotos Eaters can't be quite successful in life. They can rise to the top on their skills as conciliators and compromisers, which come naturally; they have no problem putting their own position aside. They can be especially fine counselors of the client-centered persuasion, because it is easy for them to focus on someone else's journey. They are likely to be modest and even-tempered, unassuming and non-judgmental. With a strong boss or a willful spouse a Lotos Eater can be the perfect foil, the person who knows how to get out of the way. On a team immobilized by conflict, they can be the peacemaker.

Dwight Eisenhower was a genial, self-effacing Lotos Eater who was chosen Supreme Allied Commander not to be the grand strategist of World War II — he mainly left strategy to others — but because he was able to manage the conflicting egos of the likes of General George S. Patton and Field Marshal Bernard Law Montgomery; Eisenhower kept his own ego out of the way.

Even as U.S. president, Eisenhower described himself as a "middle of the roader" who neither increased nor decreased existing federal programs, and did not particularly initiate new policies. His strategy was that of the Lotos Eater: to avoid the fray, not to rock the boat, to maintain the *status quo*, to be agreeing and agreeable without actually doing much. The country muddled along.

This sloggy, suburban consciousness of the 1950s in America, pleasant but also banal, is the consciousness of Lotos Land. When John Kennedy ran to succeed Ike, Kennedy's slogan, in response to the Lotos-induced torpor, was "Let's get America moving again!"

## Lotos Lands

Lotos eating is the familiar culture of slow-moving bureaucracies and large institutions. Plodding organizations like the postal service, ponderous government agencies, insurance companies, and public utilities are set up with routines, precedents and procedures *not to make decisions,* which are so difficult for Lotos Eaters, *but to let the decisions make themselves.*

The by-word is to go with the flow of paperwork, not to make waves or disrupt the routine. There is little taste for disagreement or confrontation. Initiative is frowned upon. Like a big oil tanker in the water, a massive effort is required to get started in new directions. And once Lotos Eaters build up a head of steam, they just operate on momentum.

## Accedia

The resignation of the Lotos Eaters is more than sad, it's a *deadly sin* which the desert fathers, early Christian monastics, called *accedia*, sloth, (despondency, lethargy, discouragement) the sin of not caring (Gr., *a*=not, *kedos*=care). The Lotos Eaters just don't care.

The philosopher Alanus said *accedia* was "the torpor of the mind by which one either neglects to begin good works or grows weary in them." Theologian Matthew Fox calls *accedia* "couch-potato-itis." And, remembering that lotos is the goo at the beginning of Odysseus' journey to be most himself, Søren Kierkegaard called accedia "the despairing refusal to be oneself."

The only antidote for *accedia* — not caring — is to serve your desire. Desire is served only when you let it affect you, disturb you, demand of you, when you let it shake you up. You can't use lotos to dull desire and avoid the journey.

The choice to attend to one's desires, in a hard world where the small pleasures of lotos are no small matter, means the adventure has begun.

## Rowing

*"Sal, we gotta go and never stop going 'til we get there."*
*"Where're we going, man?"*
*"I don't know but we gotta go."*
— KEROUAC, *ON THE ROAD*

Once he has retrieved his lotos-drugged sailors, Odysseus lashes them to the rowing benches. With the remaining teetotalling crew, they furiously begin to paddle.

Odysseus' abrupt departure says he is not going to wait for "the right moment" or "the right people" to get going. He doesn't wait for "inspiration." He doesn't try to "get settled." He doesn't need "more information." He doesn't wait to get all his ducks in a row. These are for later.

Rowing is highly significant for what it is not. There's not much time for ruminating or navel gazing on the rowing bench. You have to keep up: you can be neither too enthusiastic nor too diffident. You can't drift aimlessly like Lotos Eaters; rowing is the opposite of going with the flow. And of most consequence: you have to put your oar in the water, just what Lotos Eaters will not do.

Thus the journey begins neither with a burst of enthusiasm nor a detailed plan. The enthusiasm will fade; the plans are of little use as the details of the journey are not yet known.

Odysseus is lost. He does not even have a map. All he has is a profound desire to get Home, and, luckily, a fleet of ships to get him there. And all he knows is he has to be in the sea and rowing — to commit to the journey — in spite of the seductions of lotos.

What is your lotos? What delicious but false comfort keeps you just where you are, unwilling to get started?

It is unlikely to be some great secret. Most people, if you asked them, could tell you right away what their lotos-of-choice is.

**You'll know you're in Lotos Land when:**

- You are in the land of inertia, stagnation and overwhelm, loss of will and desire.
- The natives create easy harmony and calm, complacency and conformity.
- Priority-setting and ambition are avoided.
- Change feels overwhelming.
- Initiative, innovation and risk-taking are discouraged.
- Decision-making is slow and bureaucratic: choices are chewed over endlessly.
- The goals (and the organizing vision) are fuzzy.
- Everything runs out of habit and on automatic.
- Disruptive, paradigm-busting talk is disapproved. Better to go with the conventional wisdom. Don't upset the apple cart.
- Deep feelings — anger and desire — are stifled.
- People are urged to accommodate, "to love what you have."

**If you are in Lotos Land:**

- Keep the memory of Home conscious: remember who you really are and who you are supposed to become.
- Keep your eyes on the prize; don't be distracted by the inessential.
- Be willing to tolerate the discomfort of *desire.*
- Be a bold self-starter, don't wait for permission or consensus, risk action instead. (There are other realms on the journey where the opposite is true).
- Put your oar in the water, even though the path toward Home may not be totally clear. This *Odyssey* begins with an existential act: Odysseus puts his oar in the water and starts rowing.

Odysseus escapes Lotos Land because his instincts are to act, to overcome obstacles and solve problems. (Other predicaments will require different escape routes.) He is not seduced by this lotos-induced, torpid state of tranquility, without elation or depression. Here in Lotos Land the way out is not through disengagement.

To the contrary, Odysseus' triumph emerges out of his longings and his *passions* — particularly his desire to be on the road home and his passion for his extraordinary wife — and his willingness to risk *engagement* on the road to get there, and to suffer the consequences.

But how much engagement is enough, and how much is too much? The next adventure with the monstrous Cyclops seeks to answer these questions.

CHAPTER TWO

# The Cyclops
# Polyphemus Perversity

*Beneath the decent façade of consciousness with its disciplined moral order and its good intentions lurk the crude instinctive forces of life, like monsters of the deep — devouring, begetting, warring endlessly. They are for the most part unseen, yet on their urge and energy life itself depends: without them living beings would be as inert as stones. But were they left to function unchecked, life would lose its meaning…as in the teeming world of primordial swamps.*

— ESTHER HARDING, *PSYCHIC ENERGY*

Odysseus comes now to an island that is an unspoiled natural paradise. The locals are the enormous giant Cyclopes, "man mountains" Homer calls them; they have one huge eye in the center of their forehead. The Cyclopes don't farm their land; instead they "live on such wheat, barley, and grapes as grow wild without any kind of tillage."[6] Cyclopes Land is a kind of Garden of Eden, a bountiful, fecund, natural wilderness.

The Cyclopes have no laws and no meeting places because each Cyclops "is lord and master in his family, and they take no account of their neighbours."[7] The Cyclopes want what they want when they want it, and they take it. They don't suffer shame or guilt or reservations. They're not worried about what others think.

Odysseus and his men make their way to the cave of a Cyclops named Polyphemus, who is out. They build a fire and make themselves at home.

When the ugly, enormous Polyphemus returns to the cave, Odysseus and his men are understandably terrified and cower in the back of the cave. Polyphemus closes his cave's opening with a huge rock slab so big that Odysseus guesses 22 wagons could not budge it.

Then Polyphemus notices his intruders. Odysseus is normally a pretty slick talker, but here he is petulant and demanding. Odysseus warns Polyphemus that Zeus himself is the god who protects travelers, so Polyphemus *had better* treat him well or else. Further, Odysseus insolently demands a "guest gift" per Greek custom.

As it happens, Odysseus has said the wrong thing in the wrong place to the wrong monster. Here in the wilds of Cyclopes Land, the customs and practices of civilized society don't apply. Odysseus wants this primal bad guy to please respect the conventions of Greek etiquette. Maybe Odysseus is scared; but have you ever been hassled by an unruly street punk, and you righteously try to shame him into being nice? It seldom works.

Polyphemus roars, 'Stranger, you are a fool, or you know nothing of this country. Fear the gods? We Cyclopes do not care about your blessed gods, for we are ever so much stronger than they!"[8] Polyphemus is a law unto himself, like any self-respecting

Cyclops. He's not afraid of Zeus, and he doesn't give a tootle about the social graces.

In a rage, and to second the point, Polyphemus crushes the heads of two of Odysseus' men and eats them raw. Then, arrogantly, supremely overconfident, he goes to sleep, even with Odysseus and his team cowering about the cave. He sleeps on his back, his feet splayed out, snoring.

Odysseus wants to run Polyphemus through with his sword straight away, but he understands — *brilliantly* — that he and his men by themselves won't be able to move the immense rock slab that imprisons them in the cave. Odysseus needs to have the Cyclops open the door.

But how? When faced with a Cyclops, the great task is to figure out a way to turn his overwhelming power to your own great purposes, to get him to move the slab for you without getting yourself eaten. It is an *aikido* (a martial art wherein you *align with* your opponent's power and momentum rather than matching him strength-for-strength.) Success here requires patience for the right moment, discipline in execution, and the rare self-sophistication that allows you not to get so hooked by your ego that you must kill him or be killed by him.

All of these Odysseus has in spades.

For a quick instant breakfast, the Cyclops scoffs two more men. When Polyphemus heads out with his flocks leaving Odysseus and his men imprisoned in the cave, they spend the day sharpening a large olivewood stake as a weapon.

Polyphemus returns in the evening to dine on two more men. Now the Cyclops asks Odysseus his name. Famously, presciently, Odysseus says his name is "Nobody."

Odysseus offers the Cyclops some potent Maronian wine[9] that he has brought with him, and in short order Polyphemus passes out *shikkered*.

This Cyclops does not know when to stop. And this is true of all Cyclopes you may meet: in spite of how big and scary they are, their voracious appetites, and their insensitivity to their own limits make them vulnerable and set up the conditions for their undoing.

Odysseus and his crew now thrust the olivewood stake through the sleeping Polyphemus's single eye. Polyphemus screams so loud in pain that he rouses his Cyclops neighbors who come running. "Polyphemus!" they yell through the slab door, "is anyone bothering you?" "Nobody!" says Polyphemus, referring to Odysseus, "Nobody is messing with me!" To which the Cyclopedian neighbors reply, "OK, if nobody's bothering you, it must be the gods at work and we'll go home." And they do.

There is more than pre-Socratic slapstick at work here. Homer offers a fundamental clue about how to deal with the Cyclops when you are besieged, overpowered and without recourse. He is saying that you have to confront the Cyclops as "Nobody," meaning that in the face of overwhelming power you act without ego. You don't proclaim to your captor who you are ("Don't you know who I am, officer?!") as Odysseus does at first. You don't demand your rights. It will only make things worse.

Most of all, you don't put up your dukes and engage him head-on, toe-to-toe, *mano a mano*. Not to a Cyclops. You don't engage the Cyclops directly and beat him by overpowering him (unless you are a Cyclops yourself). You will lose, guaranteed (as we shall see). Power is his thing. When you're in a fight with a Cyclops, and you make it personal or make it about your ego, you're surely done.

When the blinded Polyphemus opens the cave slab in the morning so that his flock can graze, Odysseus and his men escape by clinging to the underbellies of the sheep and goats, while Polyphemus pats his animals' backs but not their undersides to check for the visitors. (Another clue: The Cyclops in your life generally will not think of looking under the surface; they are not so psychological.)

Outside the cave, the crew runs for the ships and quickly casts off. But from his ship as he's sailing away, Odysseus taunts the Cyclops. "Cyclops, if any one asks you who it was that put your eye out and disgraced you, say it was the valiant warrior Odysseus, who lives in Ithaca."

Odysseus has gotten caught up in the ever-escalating cycle of revenge and one-upsmanship that is a basic feature of Cyclops lands everywhere; he cannot resist sticking it one more time to the Cyclops. But now the Cyclops goes him one better.

Once Odysseus reveals his true name, Polyphemus can ask for a specific revenge. The Cyclops prays to his father, the Lord of the Sea Poseidon, that Odysseus never reach home, or if he must return, that he arrive a broken man after a long struggle, in a foreigner's ship, and find lots of trouble at home.

Poseidon hears his blinded son's prayer and, furious for revenge, he singles out Odysseus for a devastating vendetta that will last the next ten years. Odysseus does ultimately make it Home (not to give away the ending), but Polyphemus' prayer is answered: Odysseus arrives late, battered and alone; all his shipmates are dead, and he's facing very acute trouble at Home.

## The Cyclops

The Cyclops embodies the forces of nature unrestrained, uncultivated, unfettered. He is natural, raw power. He appears in the outer world as the overbearing boss, the tyrannical gang leader, the oppressive parent, wherever bullying, overwhelming might or demand or craving works its way.

In the inner world he is the "I want what I want when I want it" monster, which Carl Jung called the *libido*, and Sigmund Freud called the *id*.[10]

The id, according to Freud, is "the dark, inaccessible part of our personality, filled with energy reaching it from the instincts, but it has no organization, produces no collective will, but only a striving to bring about the satisfaction of instinctual needs."[11]

Just like the Cyclops, the id has no laws, no meeting places, no community, no sense of propriety or concern for any neighbor. The id, bursting with energy, just cares about its own will and its own pleasure.

"[A] desire or impulse which is unchecked by any kind of authority, moral or otherwise," Jung wrote, "libido is appetite in its natural state."[12] It is, he said, "the instinctual ground from which our consciousness springs."

Libido is psychic energy, the natural urge of life, the creative force that interacts with the world. Not enough libido, and you do not have enough thrust to make your mark. You are a wimp.

Too much libido means excessive craving for sensate worldly experience, the deadly sin called lust. Lust is, as psychiatrist Claudio Naranjo writes, "a passion for excess, a passion that seeks intensity, not only through sex, but in all manner of stimulation: activity, anxiety, spices, high speed, the pleasure of loud music and so on."[13] It is over-stimulation: too much, too soon, too loud, too often.

The One-Eyed Giants have many excesses and no taboos. They even go so far as to diss the Olympians: they claim to be stronger than the gods, they have contempt for the laws and conventions of society, they munch on humans, the Cyclops drinks 'til he drops, and the tale suggests the chilling possibility of improper intimacies amongst these backwoods, mountain families. Whatever they do, they press the limits, and break them. They are antisocial characters indeed.

As a condition of being human, we all must meet the Cyclops in our lives. They are usually big and loud. They can be terrible bullies, abusive, raging, intimidating forces of nature who run over you, without guilt or remorse. They see the world the same way Polyphemus does: it's a power game pure and simple, in which the strong survive. The Cyclopes choose to survive.

## One Eye

The Cyclops has just the one eye. The most particular thing that happens when you have one eye is that you lose the perception of depth, which is to say you lose the perspective of the psyche. (The Greeks thought that of the two eyes, one looked out on the external world and the other looked within. The Cyclops has no "in sight.") Without being able to look within (to see with depth) its difficult to know who you are, what's important and what to value. It's hard to see yourself in context, and with just the one eye, it's hard to see from the point of view of others.

Uninterested in complexity or reflection, neither tentative nor nuanced, Cyclopes are steamrollers who plow straight ahead over anything in their way. They don't have much flair for lateral thinking or for finessing around a problem. A Cyclops general's original plan for fighting in Iraq was simply to head straight on, guns a-blazing, directly at the Iraqi forces, but military strategists insisted on a more sophisticated flanking action.

All Cyclopes by their nature and physiology intensely focus on the one thing right in front of them; it is their great advantage and a principal source of their demise. With limited peripheral vision, the Cyclops is easily blindsided. Subtlety, cleverness, out-of-the-box thinking, misdirection, paradox? The versatility of a man of many turns? The Cyclops is not likely to see these coming.

Of course his laser focus serves the Cyclops well where intense raw power, force of will and single-mindedness are key to victory. They are not worriers because they don't see the pitfalls at the side of the road that might give pause to the average traveler.

They are willing to take the heat and run the show. They are willing to have an impact on events.

Indeed, Cyclopes are the ultimate *shtarkers*, beings who feel *comfortable* with the broad, bold exercise of power. As primal forces of nature, they enjoy a characteristic, easy (and enviable) *dominion* over their universe. With, as we know, little worry for what the gods might think, they are comfortable reshaping the world.

Cyclopes are famous as grand wheeler-dealers and empire builders, captains of industry and robber barons. They develop real estate, excavate, build buildings and bridges. And they enjoy blowing them up, too. They will, like the Corps of Engineers, redirect rivers and move mountains that block their intentions; and they will blast their own road even though they may leave bodies in their wake.

Big oil and those insatiable media mega-conglomerates attract Cyclopes (among others), and of course professional football and armed forces around the world, where crushing, decisive, sometimes ruthless, action is required. As with Polyphemus, they are not racked with guilt or immobilized by pussyfooting sensitivity to the concerns of others.

The Cyclops is the opposite of everything ethereal, woo-woo, new age, "spiritual," otherworldly. He is carnal and disgusting. He kills and eats Odysseus' men, and then he vomits them up. He drools his wine. He has his eye poked out with a stick. It is all messy, gruesome, horrible.

In rough and tumble Cyclops Land, problems are resolved not by talking them through, but by direct confrontation and by the knocking of heads (as Polyphemus knocks the heads of Odysseus' men against the cave wall). The social niceties are honored in the breach.

As such, the encounter with the Cyclops is not *theoretical* (Gr. *theoros*, spectator). This is not the place for concern with larger moral issues and grandiloquent reflections on the uses and abuses of power.

No. Working with a Cyclops means getting your hands dirty and likely bloody. Those who succeed here will need a strong ego, a down-to-earth bent and the predilection to break some eggs to make an omelet. Audacity, even brazenness is required. You must be *willing* and then *able* to affect the real world, the visible and tangible, to mix it up, to leave your mark.

A team of rescuers heading into an emergency can't fuss too much about their environmental impact, or take the time to consider the philosophical implications of their work.

The politically correct, the terminally empathic, those so umbrageous about imposing their views or themselves, need not apply; they will die here. Polyphemus' cave is littered with the bones of well-meaning travelers who virtuously tried to rise above confrontation, and of the squeamish who just collapse in the face of temporal power.

The principal concern in Cyclops Land is always *strategic*: how to get out of the ogre's cave, given that he is a big monster and you are (likely) not. In order to make it, you must be conscious of *how your power really works* in your life. Invariably the threatening Cyclops forces his adversaries to deal with their own self-deceptions or reservations or guilt about how they *really* act with power in the world.

How comfortable are you with your own powers?

Groups and teams usually meet the Cyclops early in their process; sometimes this group stage is called "storming"[14] where the power relations and the pecking order are worked out. Who's in charge of what? Who is a big deal on this team, and who is a small deal?

A group can kill its Cyclops or let it run wild. When a group tames its Cyclops the relations are too formal and dry, perhaps with a rigid system of protocols; the group has no juice to be a force in their world, no libido. But when a group's Cyclops runs wild, the group members, like Polyphemus and his cohorts, are each a law unto himself; the result can be a cacophonous anarchy.

### What shall we do with the drunken Cyclops?

What to do when you meet the Cyclops in his cave? There are two obvious choices for Odysseus. He can kill the Cyclops, or he can let the monster eat him.

### If Odysseus kills the Cyclops

If Odysseus kills the Cyclops, he makes a big mistake. With the Cyclops dead, Odysseus can't move the stone slab. He will die in the cave.

Sometimes people who meet their Cyclops/libido are so shocked at its boldness and lack of propriety that they try like Odysseus to shame it into shaping up, into following the rules and honoring convention. (When Odysseus meets Polyphemus he impotently demands that the Cyclops be polite and fear the gods.)

But the Cyclops won't be shamed, and he won't change. So some make the choice that Odysseus does not: while the Cyclops sleeps, they kill him.

These righteous Cyclops slayers feel justified: after all, the Cyclops is a bad fellow with a bad temper and bad breath, and he must be brought under control. He's a cannibal, he's loud, he's impolite. He may have weapons of mass destruction. He must be taught a lesson whatever the cost.

Some people who kill their Cyclops are sanctimonious and tightly wound, like a fire and brimstone preacher more interested in a Pyrrhic victory — in being right — than in the practical necessity to get out of the cave alive. Other Cyclops killers may be philosophers or theorists who observe life safely from the sidelines, maybe commenting or analyzing; for whatever reason, they don't want to have to mix it up with the gritty, earthly ogre.

But however they do it, people who kill (or bury away) their interior Cyclops devastate their ability to act with effective power in the world. Without the Cyclops to open the cave slab, they sentence themselves to impotence, to a slow death in the cave.

With no Cyclops/libido, there is no lust for life, for building and creating, for experiencing pleasure or joy, and most especially, for making your mark on earth. People who kill the Cyclops don't make the journey Home; whatever their self-righteous justification for killing the Cyclops, their future ends sanctimoniously in the Cyclops' cave.

In the now almost forgotten brouhaha that was the American presidential election of 2000, Albert Gore, Jr. tried desperately to suppress his Cyclops during the rough and tumble recounts in Florida.

The Gore side had a variety of colorable challenges to the victory of then Texas Governor G.W. Bush in Florida. But Gore declined to pursue these messy fights, a catastrophic choice in the Land of the Cyclops.

Writes lawyer Jeffrey Toobin: "Gore's analytical powers were such that he even convinced himself not to make the very claims that might have won him the election in an honorable way. If Bill Clinton was a prisoner of his id, Gore was bedeviled by his superego — an internal censor so strong that it wiped out not only the killer instinct but also the fighting spirit."[15]

Gore did not contest even those battles where most observers considered that he had both the law and the facts on his side. He was reportedly worried about what people would think and about the judgments of history; but for whatever reason, he wouldn't engage his earthly ogre; he wanted to be righteously above the battle. He put the *kibosh* on his own Cyclops, immobilizing himself.

Meanwhile, the Republicans precisely understood that they were in Cyclops Land. "While the Vice-President [Gore] and his aides were hunched over their calculators," Toobin continues, "the Republicans were breaking bar stools over their heads."[16]

## If the Cyclops kills Odysseus

If, on the other hand, the Cyclops kills Odysseus, then the libido takes over the controls. The Cyclops comes and goes from the cave as he pleases. Life then is indeed about excessive, unrestrained appetites: meeting cravings and lusts as they appear, whatever the consequences.

The Cyclops are *id*-iots — big, loud bullies who want their own way, who only see their own way, and who will run over others to get it. The Cyclop's life is a series of showdowns and intimidations.

President Lyndon B. Johnson was a Cyclops; he was famous for his *physically* intimidating, in-your-face, arm-twisting as he pressed his case. (Physical intimidation is a favorite Cyclops tactic.) He stood too close, he talked too loudly, he drilled his finger into his listener's solar plexus. He famously, outrageously, took meetings, even with his vice-president, in his bathroom, taunting propriety as all Cyclopes will do. He shamelessly bent or broke the election laws while running for office in Texas, stealing at least one election for the Senate; he was a Cyclops testing the limits.

The record is now clear that Johnson as president knew early on that he could not win the war in Vietnam, but even so, he did not withdraw. As a Cyclops, the only option he could see was to plow straight ahead, ramp up the volume of men and armaments, to turn up the power to dramatic but unfulfilling excess. It was the enemy who, with cleverness and misdirection, turned the Cyclops' overwhelming power to their own purposes.

## The Third Way

Rather than killing the Cyclops or being killed by him, Odysseus takes The Third Way, which is difficult because it balances instinct with self-discipline, a sophisticated highwire act. Odysseus *wounds* but does not kill the Cyclops. He shows the monster who's boss, and then cleverly, adroitly, tricks the Cyclops into opening the door, to use his great strength in the service of Odysseus' journey.

If you learn the lessons of the Cyclops' cave you can act gracefully with power in the world. You are not fooled by either extreme: neither are you overwhelmed, immobilized and afraid to act with muscle; nor are you a Cyclops out of control and with only the "power on" button to push.

Why does someone get stuck in the Cyclops' cave? *It is always a failure of imagination about power;* the traveler is afraid of it or consumed by it. Travelers mired on the Cyclopes Island are struggling with how power works in their own lives: how to be bold and also graceful, how to be neither a wimp nor a bully. If someone seems particularly powerful or particularly weak — where questions of asserting their will, the direct expression of anger, and dominion over their own world are central — they are sure to be working with Cyclops energy.

Consider Plato's example of the wild horse named Appetite. (It is unrestrained appetite for experience that drives the Cyclops.) If you let Appetite run wild under you, it goes where it wants and isn't much help on your journey. Or you can kill the horse and sit comfortably on the carcass without worrying too much about the horse throwing you off. Alas, the horse won't be able to take you where you want to go. But if you channel the horse's power without breaking its spirit — a creative tension between raw instinct and the civilized restraints of life that each traveler must resolve for himself through a conscious relationship with his Cyclops — then you continue on your journey.

Odysseus' commendable *metis* (practical wisdom) aside, it is Polyphemus' own one-eyed, one-sided distorted view of reality that ultimately does him in.

First, the giant thinks he is invulnerable. Odysseus and his men are left free to wander about the cave, both during the day when they do the mischief of creating a weapon and also at night, when the Cyclops falls sound asleep with no sense of alarm.

*The Cyclops feels invulnerable because he concentrates on his own strengths:* that he is big and strong and on his own turf where he has dominion. Yet to an astonishing (and fatal) degree he is oblivious to his considerable vulnerabilities: that he is naïve compared to the sophisticated Odysseus, that he is not so clever, that he thumbs his nose at the gods, and perhaps worst of all that he doesn't know when to stop, as with the heady Maronian wine.

Second, the Cyclops sees Odysseus' vulnerabilities but *he seems to think that Odysseus is without any powers or resources.* Odysseus is relatively puny, but the Cyclops overlooks the great man's considerable strengths: his inimitable intelligence and resourcefulness, his astonishing talent as a strategist, and his unshakable desire to get on with his heroic journey no matter what. In the face of Polyphemus' contempt, Odysseus remembers his own true powers. This saves him.

The Cyclops will not respect your credentials or your status. Nor will he recognize your personal qualities: your strengths, your intelligence, your depth of character, your commitment to virtue. Inevitably, and with laser accuracy, he will exploit your weaknesses, the places where you feel puny, powerless against authority or restriction.

How to outsmart the Cyclops? The trick, always, is an *aikido:*

- To work with the Cyclops as a partner, even though he may not realize it, and even though you may get your hands dirty
- *To hold faith in your own powers even as he does not*
- To engage him not on his terms and agenda but on your own
- To do your work on *the periphery of his vision* where he cannot see, and *under the obvious* where the Cyclops is not so skillful
- Use his superior, brute strength to set you free and serve your journey.

The Cyclops adventure stirs truly disturbing questions. How are your relations with the Cyclops? Do you demand (impotently) that he be polite, kept in the cave? Do you want to be above the earthly fray, as a matter of "spiritual" principle? Or the opposite: Do you let him — the inner or outer Cyclops — run things completely, the wild man gone wild? The central issue with a Cyclops is always how you can use his muscle for your own purposes.

## You'll know you're in Cyclops Land when:

- You feel powerlessness in the face of an intimidating bully who seems to hold all the cards. (Maybe it is a nasty boss, or a street tough).
- The Cyclops has real power which can crush you and which, at the same time, you are dependent upon (like a parent, or a partner, or, perhaps, a godfather.)
- The Cyclops does not see who you really are: your considerable strengths, your commitment to virtue, the private struggles you endure.

- You despair about your own powers, whether they are real or of any value.

**If you meet the Cyclops:**

- Don't try to reason. Reason is out of place here.
- Don't demand your rights. The customs of civil society don't apply either.
- Don't moralize or threaten the gods' retribution. The Cyclops is not religious. He's not afraid of the Olympians.
- You can be sure the Cyclops will test the limits and break the rules, conventions, laws and understandings (especially if *you* are the person setting the rules).
- He is guaranteed to test *you* as well, to see what you are made of, to see if you are, as Polyphemus asks Odysseus, a pirate or a trader, and, more to the point, whether you are a man or a mouse. Much as Polyphemus eats Odysseus' men at will, any Cyclops will begin to chomp away at that which you are in charge of, whether it be your employees (undermining your authority) or your areas of responsibility, or he will encroach upon your basic rights and prerogatives that you thought were insured by convention and the powers that be (as Odysseus thought his rights as a traveler were secured by Zeus). He will press the boundaries to see what your limits are, and what you will do, the way a small boy might poke at an insect.
- Remember to work from your own powers, even though the Cyclops will try to make you think you don't have any.
- Don't retaliate out of anger or loss of temper. Have a tempered, clever (*metis*-ful) plan instead. A calm head is the way to deal with the wild man.
- Don't take on the Cyclops face-to-face, on his terms. Don't take the bully by the horns. You will lose for certain.

Rather, the Cyclops' great vulnerability is to indirection. Like Odysseus, speak cleverly to power.

- Set clear limits but don't raise the level of confrontation. You need to stand up to the bullying Cyclops, but you can't kill him or be killed by him, or you will be stuck in the Cyclops mindset forever. You will die in the cave under the misimpression that life is simply about raw, brutal, direct power.

## The Poseidon Adventure

Once Odysseus reveals his true identity, Polyphemus prays to his father Poseidon, Lord of the Sea, to take revenge against Odysseus.

Poseidon superintends a vast, primitive oceanic kingdom, which is below the surface, under conscious awareness. The *deep* is his domain. It is dark and unfathomable, a Mystery. It is a world that we do not know: normally we only skim the surface.

Poseidon bullyrags us with messages from the deep however he chooses: with neurotic symptoms, depressions, shocks and failures of whatever kind. The Sea God is around when we feel as though we're inundated, in over our head, overwhelmed, swept away by sea changes. He can be turbulent and destructive: he devises earthquakes, volcanoes and typhoons. He makes waves. He rocks the boat, whatever it takes to unnerve a traveler.

Oh, Poseidon certainly makes the journey home perilous and fraught with difficulty; he is vengeful and mischievous and relentless, at critical moments scuttling Odysseus' best laid plans.

But with his tests he gives the journey meaning. By ensuring that Odysseus make the essential detours and meet the necessary beings, he transports Odysseus to worlds beyond himself. And Poseidon teaches Odysseus profound lessons in what may be the main thing for a traveler: the depth of his resources to continue.

These are hard lessons, tough love. Every lesson is crucial for the self-involved, full of himself, sorry for himself, easily distracted Odysseus.

Still Poseidon seems to thoroughly enjoy his grudge and most people cast moody, volatile Poseidon as the bad actor in this story; yet he has every opportunity to drown Odysseus in the ocean, but he does not. Why not put the poor human out of his misery?

Poseidon will not let Odysseus off the hook so easily. Later, the soothsayer Tiresias and the goddess Circe tell Odysseus that his harrowing trials will not end until he makes his peace with Poseidon. The god of the depths *insists* that Odysseus come to terms with him. But what will it take? *What does Poseidon want?*

This is the decisive question, of course. But for now, as Poseidon insinuates himself into Odysseus' journey, the story becomes the Sea God's as well. Somehow, and to some purpose, these two, man and god, are traveling companions of a kind.

CHAPTER THREE

# Aeolus
# The Wind Done Gone

*Nothing can be known*
*unless it first appears as a psychic image.*
— C.G. JUNG

*Man's reach must exceed his grasp,*
*else what's a heaven for?*
— ROBERT BROWNING

Next Odysseus reaches Aeolia, home of Aeolus, who is Master of the Winds. Aeolia is an island that floats whimsically on the sea with no fixed location; it bobbers wherever the winds blow it.

The Aeolians live lightly, playfully, spontaneously. Each day they enjoy an elegant party with food and music. The conversation is witty, bubbly and sophisticated. They have every conceivable kind of luxury. And at night, according to Odysseus, they sleep with their mates on lavish, ornate bedsteads.

The Aeolians, says Odysseus, "feast on *without end."* Not only is the party ongoing, but the Aeolians also have the optimist's sense that it will *never* end, like the partygoers on Wall Street or in Silicon Valley in the 1990's.

But Odysseus and his men want to get home, and not just party.

Still, even the most sober traveler could not ignore the fun, lightness and excitement, the great spirit of the place. The crew parties-on for a full month.

And as Odysseus prepares to leave, Aeolus presents him with a magical gift: an ox-skin inside of which he has tied all the winds except for Zephyr, the West Wind, which was left free to blow Odysseus and his crew home to Ithaca.

With Zephyr at their back, in nine days they are at last so close to home that Odysseus can see Ithaca, he can see the shepherds tending fires, so close that he has a bird's eye view of the island in sharp detail, and he must be beyond joy. He can smell it, and he can taste it. It is a spectacular, *numinous* vision of home, just what he had hoped. It is what the psychologist Abe Maslow would have called a peak experience; and it is as high as Odysseus will get, and as close as he will get to Home, until he actually makes it to Ithaca nine years from now. (You might say it is a "peek experience:" Aeolus gives Odysseus a good look at what might be.)

But now Odysseus tires and dozes off, a sign that something imaginal is happening, that his normal waking consciousness can't contain or process events. Who would not be overwhelmed, *glutted,* by such a clear and close vision of the end of his long journey?

Sorry to say, with Odysseus fast asleep, the crew starts to talk amongst themselves, muttering that Aeolus has surely stuffed the ox-skin (which holds the winds) with silver and gold and treasure for Odysseus alone. Upset that they might be cheated, the impudent, imprudent crew breaks the bag open. They are looking for a *windfall,* and they get it. All the winds escape and the furious whirlwind blasts them right back to Aeolia.

> *"With their silver and gold*
> *they make idols for themselves...*
> *They sow the wind and reap the whirlwind"*
> — Hosea 7:8

Back on Aeolia, a devastated Odysseus humbly approaches Aeolus for a second wind, but Aeolus declines: If the gods detest you that much, pal, you're not getting any help from me. Aeolus doesn't need a weatherman to know which way the winds are blowing. He does not like bad vibes at all, and in the face of them he is surprisingly cold-hearted, dismissive and cynical. The bright, fun, playful, helpful consciousness of Aeolus that Odysseus left behind has already floated away by the time of the blowback. Aeolus is in "another place" now.

And Odysseus is left holding the (wind) bag.

There comes a time in life when you know where you want to go, you get *wind* of it. You can *imagine* it. This is the time to pay your respects to dazzling Aeolus who can inspire, clarify and refine the vision: he lets the winds of the imagination propel you to where you want to go — so that you can see what it would be like if your dreams were to come true, so that you can see what Ithaca looks like. Aeolia is *the* place to envision Home.

The central, salient feature of Aeolia is that it is not tied down. It is a (psychological) place with "no fixed location."

Thus Aeolians are always available for wherever the latest breeze takes them; rootless, they can easily, and without the slightest embarrassment or apology, reverse direction on a whim, and then do it again; consistency is not remotely a concern. Everything is negotiable. They keep their options and opportunities perpetually open.

Aeolia is an ideal place for innovation and improvisation, for taking risks and for experimenting with new ideas. Aeolians are imaginative thinkers *because* they are not wedded to the conventional wisdom; they are not bound by "where they were" in the past. They naturally think outside the boxes that others are wedged in.

We meet them as smart, charismatic, upbeat people with nimble minds, articulate generalists who can bobber from subject to subject with ease, dilettantes who deftly skim the surface. They will be drawn to the new, the cutting edge, the outré, the latest ideas. Like the floating island itself, they are not anchored to tradition, or to the past, or even to their own history; their focus is utterly on visioning the exciting and new that is just out of reach.

Aeolus' special gift is to help the traveler strategize and imagine what is yet to come, and to that he adds his particular brand of spirited enthusiasm; as with our hero, Aeolus gins up an extraordinary picture of what-could-be, what Ithaca would be like, just the way you imagine and hope for.

Aeolians are easily found in the vast professional economy of futurists and imagineers, in think tanks and world peace organizations, devising splendid concepts, even *spiritual* concepts — *especially* spiritual concepts — that galvanize and inspire and promise to bring everyone together in a just and good world: enthusiastic hope on a grand scale for world change, ending hunger in our lifetime and war as we know it, colonizing other planets.

But Aeolians are not so interested in whether the ideas are practical, or in the trodding and plodding *groundwork* that it will take to get there.

**What you see is not what you get**

And that is why it is impossible to get home from Aeolia. Oh, you can dream your dream house at Aeolia, and even draw up the blueprints. But a real home entails a commitment to a particular location, to holding your ground, to digging down and excavating, setting a foundation and building a solid structure. Home, Ithaca, is the opposite of keeping your options open, of following the latest breeze, of not taking responsibility for how things come out.

Whether you in fact *get* to Ithaca is obviously not Aeolus' concern: he is more interested in *the idea* of Ithaca. (If he were more concerned with results, as are the noble Phaecians down the line, he could easily have supplied our hero with further assistance.)

If you have problems with the gods, or your crew, or if there are other bumps in the road related to the practicalities, well, tough. Aeolus will not be interested in your repair (Lt, *re* – + *patria,* native country). As with Odysseus, he may get irritated or worse. Difficult personal situations are swept under the rug on this island. He plain doesn't like hassles. There is no energy for regrets or what-might-have-beens here. If your project tanks, by the time you are back to complain, he will have floated on to another place anyway.

Without a real-world strategy for reaching a goal, or because the premises themselves change so quickly, Aeolians "wing it." They launch all kinds of trial balloons and see what will "fly." They have no shortage of ideas or possibilities, and there is little reason to pre-qualify them, or nail down the details in advance, or work them through.

Long ago in Washington, DC, in a spacious, elegant antebellum mansion deep in the woods of Rock Creek Park, was the headquarters of a non-profit foundation dedicated to studying the future of society (as Aeolus offers Odysseus a vision of his future). Meetings, about grand plans to develop research projects, seminars, conferences, and the like, were constant and everywhere, in offices and hallways and nooks and crannies. Astonishing, boundary-breaking ideas zipped past.

Fancy people — academics, philanthropists, scientists, even members of Congress — happened by. Business executives had tea with Tibetan lamas. I met the visionary LSD'er Timothy Leary there, an Aeolus himself. Food was constantly being served. The charming party, as in any Aeolia, was ongoing.

Virtually all meetings and presentations were videotaped, but nobody took notes or watched the videos. There was very little follow-up.

In the end, the money ran out and the people drifted away. Left behind, as with Aeolia, were the dashed hopes of what might have been, and also the lingering ache of possibilities yet to come (*if only* they had better luck, and more funding, and a more sensible crew).

In our story, Odysseus' vision is blown away when the crew covets the imagined gold in the wind bags.

But don't blame the crew: Commonly *what looks like a sack of gold* in Aeolia, the land of possibilities, *will actually be a bag of wind.* Ask any high-tech venture capitalist or entrepreneur. The Aeolian attention naturally goes to the grandest possible upshot. Consider how companies were imaginatively valued by Aeolian promoters during the dot-com boom: by the number of hits to a website as opposed to actual sales, for example, or, as is typical of Aeolian snake oil, by the upside limit — "Do you know how many people are on the Internet!?!" — and not by the realities of the marketplace.

The suddenly vanished vision of Ithaca holds echoes of a famous episode in another winding odyssey, the young knight Parsifal's search for the Holy Grail. When Parsifal arrives early on and quite suddenly at the Grail Castle, he is welcomed by the Fisher King and the court. He celebrates a superb evening, a marvelous banquet (as also Aeolus provides). He sees and is stunned by the beauty and power of the Grail (much as Odysseus is taken with his shimmering vision of Ithaca, his own Grail). But when Parsifal awakes in the morning, the King and his courtiers are nowhere to be found, and the Grail has disappeared (as Ithaca evaporates in Odysseus' story).

Later, Parsifal is told that he lost his opportunity because he failed to ask the King the famous, essential question, "Whom does the Grail serve?" Parsifal forgot, or by some accounts was afraid or too shy to inquire about the true significance of the Grail, which is to say the import of his quest.

The question is a knotty one, and many answers to it have been proposed over the centuries. But Parsifal's real difficulty was not with the question but with the questioner. Simply put, he wasn't ready to ask. His real self wasn't ready to confront the meaning of his quest.

Odysseus makes it home, almost. He gets a crystal clear vision of his personal destiny. But why doesn't he get there? We have to assume the possibility that he is not ready to face the meaning of his journey.

*What is the significance of the Odyssey? Whom does Odysseus' journey serve? How does the journey matter?*

Well, you say, as Odysseus might at this point, it is to get back to Ithaca, to be at-home in the world and to build a life with Penelope. But what a modest thing it would be if this journey is for Odysseus' own salvation. Perhaps there is something more.

This we know for sure: Aeolus is a brilliant guide to the envisioning, but he can't help much with the meaning of the quest. Real meaning is not some clever idea floating about: it has to be unearthed, a consequence of the dust-ups that come from serious traveling.

While it's easy to get lost in Odysseus' failure to make it to Ithaca, he has pictured his home island in clear and most compelling detail. Whatever his disappointment, Odysseus knows that if it is possible to get that close, it is possible to get home. Who could say that this knowing is not essential?

### You'll know you're in Aeolia if:

- There is great focus on the big picture future.
- Ideas, imagination, and clever, leading-edge thinking are central.
- The give-and-take comes fast (Aeolus means "quick").
- Ideas and positions change with the wind.
- You celebrate a moveable feast: there is no sense of permanence or rootedness.
- The impulsive, undisciplined, glib locals skim the emotional surface.
- The culture values having fun and being upbeat.
- There is little tolerance for the downside possibilities or ideas.
- Loyalty to a company, or commitment to seeing things through, are not priorites.

### If you are in Aeolia:

- The visit to Aeolus can answer the question: What is possible?
- This is the valuable time to envision and plan and imagine the exciting future, to see how your dreams can work.
- Ask questions. Explore the widest range of possibilities. Generate alternatives. Aeolus loves hypothesizing.

- Being overwhelmed, immobilized or intoxicated by possibilities, gets you stuck in Aeolia.
- Don't confuse a good idea with practical action. Aeolus can't get you home just by helping you imagine home.
- Hard work and meeting responsibilities will get you out of this temporary place and on with the journey.

CHAPTER FOUR

# The Laestrygonians Darkness at Noon

*For the thing which I greatly feared is come upon me,*
*and that which I was afraid of is come unto me.*
— JOB 3:25

*The study of lives and the care of souls means above all*
*a prolonged encounter with what destroys*
*and is destroyed.*
— JAMES HILLMAN

*Our feigning with the strange unlike, whence springs*
*The difference that heavenly pity brings.*
— WALLACE STEVENS, "TO THE ONE OF FICTIVE MUSIC"

*We have met the enemy and he is us.*
— POGO (WALT KELLY)

*But the greatest humility can be learned from the anguish of keeping your balance in such a position: of continuing to be yourself without getting tough about it and asserting your false self against the false selves of other people.*
— MERTON

After his clear vision of home turns to thin air in Aeolia, Odysseus is understandably cautious. Aeolia is the optimistic land of dreaming your greatest dreams. But Odysseus' next stop is Laestrygonia, the land of negative expectations.

The Laestrygonian harbor has a long, narrow entrance protected by tall cliffs, like a Scandinavian fjord. Laestrygonia is hard to get in to and hard to get out of. Odysseus' squadron maneuvers through the fjord and moors deep inside the harbor, all the ships huddled together. But Odysseus discreetly ties his flagship to a rocky cliff outside the entry. In Laestrygonia, as we shall see, prudence is a virtue.

But the remarkable high light of Laestrygonia is that the sun never sets. Homer calls Laestrygonia "the land of unremitting light" because there is no night, just a brief period of twilight. Odysseus, always a man looking for an angle, muses,

*"In that country a man who could do without sleep might earn double wages, one as a herdsman of cattle, and another as a shepherd, for they work much the same by night as they do by day."*[17]

Laestrygonia is the land of the midnight sun, and some who ponder the "real world" locations of the Odyssey like to put Laestrygonia somewhere near the Arctic Circle. Like the far north in winter, Odysseus' adventure here is cold and stark and brutal.

Odysseus sends three men to scout around, and they encounter the Laestrygonians, unpleasant, unattractive giants. When they chance on the queen, she is so hideous *they hate her on sight.*

The Laestrygonian King Antiphates seizes one of the men and eats him on the spot, just like that. The two other scouts flee for the ships, but they are followed by a horde of giant Laestrygonians who, without apparent provocation, rain great boulders smashing the ships in the harbor and killing all the men, except for Odysseus' ship and men outside the harbor. Odysseus slashes the cable that ties his ship to Laestrygonia, and they sail quickly away.

With their attack, the Laestrygonians launch what during the war in Việt Nam was called a "protective reaction" strike against Odysseus' fleet: since this "enemy" armada is surely going to attack anyway, the Laestrygonians feel completely justified in shooting first.

So we know for certain that Laestrygonians have a hair trigger. They're looking for trouble, alert and on the defensive, ready to pounce. These ugly giants are paranoid. They imagine the worst.

Laestrygonians in all walks of life search for how they are going to be attacked, fretting about whether their bosses or employees or significant others will do them in; then they can justify retaliating *in advance.* Concern with the hidden motives and secret agendas of others drives the Laestrygonians.

And why does the sun never set here? It is because the Laestrygonians are afraid of the dark. They need to see what people are up to, and who can be trusted. They need to keep an eye on their enemies, and their friends, and of course each other. They are looking for proof that they are safe, but no evidence will ever suffice.

In the relentless bright light — and to the psyche bright light means the rational and scientific, the intention to understand and control, the search for clues that will predict — the Laestrygonians are confident that they see in sharp relief the dangers that they face, that they know the world as it is. But their gaze is superficial, merely on the external. With the light always on, there is no opportunity or inclination for interiority, introspection, or self-knowledge.

> *"If a man wishes to be sure of the road he travels, he must close his eyes and walk in the dark."*
> — ST. JOHN OF THE CROSS,
> *THE DARK NIGHT OF THE SOUL*

As Jung pointed out, an intense emphasis on one extreme constellates its opposite. So in Laestrygonia, in spite of, or rather because of, the constant light on "what's happening out there," we have, inevitably, considerable concern with matters that do in fact transpire in the dark: What are other people really up to? What's happening under the surface? How will I be done in?

## Us Against Them

Because Laestrygonia is unambiguously light and dark, black and white, these natives sharply divide the world into enemies and allies. Eldridge Cleaver, of the Laestrygonian Black Panthers, said, "If you are not part of the solution, you are part of the problem." There are no shades of gray in the noonday sun.

Former American president Richard Nixon was a Laestrygonian as well, trapped in a world of "us and them," fighting the lonely fight of survival against those he thought were trying to do him in. He kept an "enemies list," the perfect Laestrygonian thing to do. His searchlight was always on, scanning the dark for conspiracies and threats. He directed covert operations himself, including breaking into an enemy's psychiatrist's office, to find out what was going on in his enemy's mind, which is of course *the* central concern of *all* Laestrygonians. A true Laestrygonian, Nixon knew for certain that he had to strike his enemies preemptively, and that he was justified to do so.

**Laestrygonia**

Modern Laestrygonians by nature feel persecuted and attacked; they stay alert and well defended against enemies real and imagined. They want to know who is loyal and who is not. Inevitably, they develop intelligence capabilities.

Police agencies are famous Laestrygonias: primed for rapid response to danger, they are the good guys who are out to get the desperados. Cults, too, band together to fight the good fight against the forces of *darkness.*

The Central Intelligence Agency is Laestrygonia *par excellence*, always on the lookout, searching for information and threats and hidden intentions, wondering what enemies and friends are up to, assuming the worst, ready and anxious to pounce on intruders.

Each of us has our own inner Laestrygonia, a private CIA, a land of doubt and worry. We doubt other people, their motives, competence and allegiances. How will I be done in? Can I trust others? *And most of all*, we doubt ourselves and our abilities and our authority to act.

The King of the Laestrygonians is named, astonishingly, Antiphates — "opposed to recognition." To the extent that you choose at this point in your journey to recognize your true self, your powers, your authenticity, your depth, and particularly your authority, Antiphates, opposed to such recognition, proposes to do you in. His preferred method is to rain giant projectiles on you and your men.

What are these projectiles? In fact they are our own projections.

We project onto others what Jung called the shadow: the parts of ourselves, qualities or inclinations, that we don't want or like or believe, our small-mindedness and prejudices, our looming incompetence, our self-doubts and fears, unfortunate desires and resentments, our nascent immoralities, our disreputable parts, all those parts of ourselves that, like Antiphates, we refuse to recognize as parcel of our psychic community. They are whatever does not fit with our idealized self-image. The specifics may change with each person and with each person's shifts of attention.

We project the shadow so that it will seem to come from someone else, so that it is not our responsibility, so that it will seem as though it is the other person who makes small-minded judgments, is intent on bickering, while *our* thoughts and intentions are pristinely honorable.[18]

The Laestrygonians show up when you want to be seen for your true self. They throw a wrench in the works. They say "No, you are not worthy, not smart enough, not deep enough, not virtuous enough, not together enough. You're not ready." If you are stuck in Laestrygonia you will agree with them. You invalidate yourself, you blame yourself, you become your own enemy. You rain giant projectiles on yourself.

Laestrygonia stands in direct opposition to Ithaca, the place where you are *most recognized* for who you are. In that sense, Odysseus is at this moment the farthest he can be from home. Of any imbroglio, the Laestrygonians do by far the most damage to Odysseus' flotilla, in a flash destroying his entire fleet except for his flagship.

## Why not fight?

Commentators over three millennia have wondered why Odysseus, the great warrior, didn't put up a better fight with the Laestrygonians. Why isn't he more engaged, more willful, more like a hero? In fact, their huge size notwithstanding, why doesn't he run them through? After all, he handled the monstrous Cyclops pretty well.

It may seem as though Odysseus has failed. But the Laestrygonians *inevitably* serve up a chilling experience of alienation, victimization or defeat. Why? Because they are projections from the unconscious, and projections are always created to seem bigger and more powerful than their creator. You can't overpower your worst projections *on their own terms.* The criminal element seems just a little more than the police can handle, the foreign terrorists slightly too problematic for the CIA, the devil always threatens even the strongest cult's existence.

By fleeing, Odysseus withdraws from his self-invalidating projections. He survives because he does not engage the Laestrygonians as they would like him to. He will not make himself at home in this paradigm, this set of paranoid perceptions about the world.

You can't beat the Laestrygonians by wrestling with them on their their own turf by their rules: you will be trapped in Laestrygonia, stuck in the *self-invalidating mindset,* negating the negators, fighting a dirty, little guerilla war that you cannot win.

Jung cautions that projections "prove almost impossible to influence." With all your arguments, you are not likely to be able to convince the Laestrygonians that they are wrong. What kills the Laestrygonians, the experts at non-recognition, is recognition of who they are (which is to say, who *you* are.) This means facing the shadow without compromise, which requires real courage.

Long ago, in the stunning Blue Ridge mountains of western Virginia, I was in training to be a counselor. The main therapeutic approach was to expose and reform the shadow.

The solution to most problems was to expose more shadow material. What are your dark intentions? How do you not mean what you say? For a Laestrygonian, the real truth is *always* hidden; and the center of the action — what really matters — is in these secrets, what is left unsaid or under the surface.

We became expert at articulating the shadow's fine points, and we developed a taste for finding these in others. We were as sophisticated about the shadow as the Eskimos are about snow.

The real predicament of the Laestrygonians is that they are too attuned to trouble, to fighting it or running from it. If you define yourself as a shadow fighter, as we did in those days, then you become a denizen of Laestrygonia: you choose to make your home in that suspicious frame of reference. In that case, the journey ends here in this miserable, unwelcoming, graceless place. As the psychoanalyst Adam Phillips writes, "If you are part of the solution, you are part of the problem."

## Courage

What to do in Laestrygonia?

In *The Republic*, Plato makes the Guardians of the City the virtuosos of courage. The way they acquire that virtue is not to eliminate the feeling of fear — a fearless person is, of course, not courageous — but rather to learn what should legitimately be feared and what should not be.

Courage means thinking clearly in situations that are dangerous, difficult, painful or scary and then acting on the resolution. Protestant theologian Paul Tillich writes that "Courage is presence of mind in the presence of fear."

The contentious, hyperalert Laestrygonians are not courageous, quite the opposite. They do not see the threats they face *in context*. All visitors are equally suspect; all dangers are potentially catastrophic. It is as if air raid sirens blow 24-hours a day, non-stop, "just in case." To the Laestrygonians, the only sensible response to visitors seems to be a full bore pre-emptive strike.

When you are attacked by the Laestrygonians, always an unpleasant situation since they target their heavy projectiles with devastating precision, you need to sort out and acknowledge what is true and what is important about their attack — they will pummel your soft spots — without being stymied by them.

You need courage to face the Laestrygonian parts of yourself, to see them for what they are, neither inflating them nor deflating them, seeing how brutal and invalidating they are but also to see them in their context, *and then to go on anyway.*

"The courage to be," wrote Tillich, "is an ethical act in which man affirms his own being in spite of those elements of his existence which conflict with his essential self-affirmation...In the act of courage, the most essential part of our being prevails against the less essential."[19] That's how you take on the Laestrygonians.

Odysseus does not try to conquer the Laestrygonians or repress them or eat them. He sees that they will not be vanquished; if he were to engage them by fighting them he would die here, as the vast majority of his sailors do, in the Laestrygonian frame of reference. He does not get hooked by them. He does not yield to their view of him.

Instead, he *recognizes* the invalidators for who they are and what they are. He sees clearly their power, their brutality, the need to dodge their invalidating, well-aimed projectiles. He sees this is not the place to make his stand; he will have to be recognized elsewhere. He takes his lumps, and he hits the road.

And here is the outcome: Odysseus faces his own demons. They have thrown him for a loop, caused him real damage, and yet he continues on. Who can say that is cowardly?

After Odysseus had the wind knocked out of him in the Aeolian adventure, and now that he's been pummeled in the Laestrygonian darkness, his dis-inflation is complete. Simply meeting the Laestrygonians in your life is reason enough for humility. Consider when you have not been "recognized" for who you really are by powerful people (or not so powerful people) who falsely accused you or misunderstood your intentions. They did not see your compassionate heart, your intelligence, your honorableness or your sophistication. So frustrating. And yet these people are just the Laestrygonians made manifest. The trick, as always, is not to settle in Laestrygonia, which is to say, not to let their dehumanizing definition of you be the one you settle for.

**You'll know you're in Laestrygonia when:**

- The world seems dangerous, the truth is hidden, and appearances are suspect.
- People are divided into enemies and allies. It is us against them, the good guys (us) against the bad guys, or so it appears.
- Reality looks black and white, with no shades of gray.
- Motives and intentions and important facts will be hidden.
- You are not affirmed for who you really are: your honorableness, your good intent, your kind heart.

**If you are in Laestrygonia:**

- Courage! Laestrygonia always demands self-affirmation in the face of dark forces who want to do you in.
- The Laestrygonians cannot be conquered or eradicated, or convinced that they are wrong.
- Don't dismiss the Laestrygonians' concerns. They may be right as far as they go.
- Recognizing them for who they are, without exaggeration, saps their power to *entrap* you.
- See the truth of their position, and also their blind spots, and then move on.

- If you fight them on their terms you will be stuck in the Laestrygonia mindset.
- Surviving a visit to Laestrygonia requires an *anchorage* ("a source of reassurance"[20]) outside the Laestrygonian harbor.
- Disclose your own self-interest. Show as much of your motives and intentions as you can. The Laestrygonians seek transparency; they want to know what is hidden.
- Make your allegiances clear. The Laestrygonians want to know that you're not going to attack them, or even better, that you're on their side.
- Fight the good fight.

Many critics over the millennia have dismissed the Laestrygonian contretemps as a pale reprise of the Cyclops episode. And the Laestrygonians and Polyphemus are indeed both oppositional monsters who like to chomp on humans.

But in teaching and intent they are opposite.

Both want to protect their turf against intruders, but the Laestrygonians magnify the dangers they see; paranoids, they make things worse than they are. Odysseus' crew is an unlikely threat to these warrior giants, yet the Laestrygonians feel compelled to mount a devastating, pre-emptive attack. They don't know how to evaluate potential problems, so they destroy everything in sight. They overestimate the enemy.

If the Laestrygonians are a bit self-doubting, the blustery Cyclops Polyphemus is too self-confident. He downplays or ignores *real* dangers: he has no idea how great a threat Odysseus is, and that Odysseus will do him in. He overvalues his own strength and undervalues that of his visitors, just the opposite of the Laestrygonians.

CHAPTER FIVE

# Hermes
# Circe
# Holy Moly

*At all times and in all places the Circe episode has been read as a moral allegory of the triumph of Wisdom.*
— GEORGE DEF. LORD[21]

*Are you a good witch, or a bad witch?*
— GLINDA THE GOOD WITCH TO DOROTHY,
*THE WIZARD OF OZ*

The disastrous dust-up in Laestrygonia is chaotic and discombobulating. The land of enemies and allies has left Odysseus with most of his sailors dead and with just one ship left from his fleet of a dozen. Odysseus must be deeply shaken, filled with despair. If he can no longer claim to be commander of a great military force, or, on these facts, even a competent leader, he must ask: Who am I anyway?

What's happening to me? How to get on track again? He will require professional help.

Circe is the Traveler's Aid, a guru, a mentor, a wisdom teacher: she is that wise being who can offer any seeker authoritative guidance about the road ahead, if she is so inclined, and if one knows how to approach her.

Circe ("hawk," as she is a sharp-eyed and unsentimental observer) is a sorceress — "with lovely braids," according to Odysseus — who lives on the bleak island of Aeaea. A dense wood hides her marble palace. Odysseus sends a scouting squad that discovers her singing and weaving; wild animals, lions and wolves, sit tamely, fawning about her.

Circe offers Odysseus' men her special homebrew of "cheese, barley and pale honey mulled in Pramnian wine, but into the brew she stirred her wicked drugs." In fact, she slips them a Mickey Finn.

The squad leader Eurylochus doesn't drink because he is suspicious, and rightfully so, but the other sailors pig out on the potion. Once they do, Circe waves her magic wand and, *higgledy-piggledy,* these men are turned into swine. Eurylochus, stunned and frightened, hightails it back to Odysseus to tell of the men transformed into pigs. Odysseus immediately realizes *something is not kosher* and heads out to investigate.

## Pig Irony

*"Moi?"*
— Miss Piggy

Why does Circe expose Odysseus' crew as pigs?

Pigs have been disparaged as gluttons for thousands of years; they are big, greedy eaters. People who overstuff themselves are called pigs.

But gluttony extends far beyond food. Pigs may be greedy for fame, or great wealth, or power. Some people crave data and information (we meet them as ivory tower intellectuals, or scientists in research and development).

From the point of view of the psyche, the most devastating piggishness is the withholding of one's self, one's feelings, one's ideas, points of view, energy, and soulful inner world. Such people may be quiet and withdrawn, avoiding life's risks and commitments. Deep within themselves, they may be observant, thoughtful, brilliantly insightful and wise, but all from an emotional distance. They don't engage. They are under Circe's spell.

I consulted with a workteam in a large government agency that was an enchanted Aeaea. Each member of the team was pretty much an expert in his or her special field, applying analysis to different regions of the world. The team was put together with the intention that the members would cross-fertilize each other's research and inspire each other.

But unlike similar work groups, these team members rarely talked to each other. There was no inclination to share their precious information, even when sharing would have been appropriate and helpful. Team members carefully protected and hoarded their own progress, and their own work. They didn't answer each others' phones, and they didn't look out for each other, not the typical behavior for this kind of team. They remained individually isolated islands, enchanted by Circe's magic.

How to know you are under Circe's spell?

Circe's pigs desperately crave what they are enchanted by — wealth or power or information — whatever they imagine will bring security and protection from the intrusive demands of the world, from being invaded by others, and from feeling exposed and uncertain. If only they store up enough of their enchantment, those under Circe's spell believe, they can avoid feeling dependent or vulnerable or obligated.

That's how you know you are under Circe's spell: you have an enchantment, and you think hoarding your enchantment will protect you and keep you safe.

*Being greedy is being enchanted.*

The enchanted are *pigheaded*, perversely obstinate and self-centered. They want things their way. They want things to stay their way. They cling too tightly to ideas about the way the world works, or should work. Stuck with their enchantment — what they believe really matters — they have a "one solution fits all" approach. What they lose is a feel for the whole and a feel for the ebb and flow of living systems.

They can't switch their frame of reference as events demand, and can't move from realm to realm on this journey. They are stuck at Circe's, forever seeking their enchantment.

Circe delights in exposing the pig in each of us, the part that refuses to be nourished. But there is a way out from being a stuck pig.

## Hermes

The Olympian god Hermes intercepts Odysseus *en route* to Circe's. The god tells Odysseus that he's in for a showdown with a powerful sorceress, and he offers up some help.

Hermes is the guide, protector and patron of travelers and boundary spanners, of those who transit from one place or realm or context to another. In fact, he often appears wearing his jaunty, wide-brimmed straw hat, and of course his famous sleek, winged sandals, as he is quite a traveler himself.

At a crossroads in ancient Greece, a traveler might add a stone to a pile of stones, called a *herm*, a puja to remember Hermes at a time of boundary crossing. He stood guard at entrances to houses and marketplaces and towns.

Whenever we are about to open a door, or enter a new understanding, a new frame of reference, when we die to one reality and are born to another, that's the time to check in with Hermes.

When the god protects important secrets, they are *hermetically* sealed. If he chooses, Hermes can break the seal and reveal the clandestine and mysterious, a process called *hermeneutics* in his honor; this is the threshold one must cross at a time of initiation, when secret information is unveiled.

That's the very boundary Odysseus must cross here at Circe's: he's as lost as lost can be. He desperately needs some information about the road ahead, some directions to home, a flash of spiritual insight.

How to invoke the god's help? How to catch his curiosity? This mischievous Olympian clearly enjoys prayers and supplications and a hearty sacrifice that are sent his way by those well-meaning travelers who want to do right by him. But Hermes is seduced by something else, not so easy for the do-gooders to gin up: it is a *shifty* attitude.

Hermes appreciates that each crossing of a border to a new realm — each initiation — requires a shift of what we pay attention to (Lt. *attendre*, to stretch to), what we believe really matters, what we value, what we are enchanted by. What really matters in one place may not be so central in another. This flex-ability to shift attention — *shiftiness* — is *the* central attribute and teaching of Hermes, god of the transitions. Hermes is allured by shiftiness, or so the stories say.

The opposite of shiftiness is *pigheadedness*. The pigheaded — those who are so stubborn in their judgment about what is ceaselessly important and valuable, the greedy who are sure that their enchantments will save them — cannot make the shift. They cannot learn about the road ahead from a teacher like Circe.

And so, as a fellow traveler with Odysseus on the back roads of the psyche, transiting from one reality to another, how shifty are you willing to be? Can you hold the idea of who you pretend to be lightly? How is the opposite of what you believe also true? If you are the sincere sort who strives to be authentic and true, can you tolerate the con?

The adventure with Circe tests these assumptions.

## Got Moly?

> *"Monks, we who look at the whole and not just the part, know that we too are systems of interdependence, of feelings, perceptions, thoughts, and consciousness all interconnected. Investigating in this way, we come to realize that there is no me or mine in any one part, just as a sound does not belong to any one part of the lute."*
>
> — SAMYUTTA NIKAYA

> *"Give not that which is holy unto the dogs,* neither cast ye your pearls before swine, *lest they trample them under their feet, and turn again and rend you."*
>
> — MATTHEW 7:6

Hermes tells Odysseus that Circe will offer him her magic potion, and when she does he must raise his sword so as to frighten her; and Hermes insists Odysseus take the magic herb called moly to neutralize (mollify) Circe's spells. Moly is a special herb — "Its root is black and its flower white as milk" — with extraordinary protective powers.

Moly's black roots and white flower are opposites, but they can't exist without each other, without cultivating each other. Moly is like the famous circular Tai Ji symbol where the opposites yin and yang — black and white, the light and dark faces of all things, the two great forces of the universe — depend upon each other in a constantly changing balance, and together make the whole.

Sometimes the components of an enterprise may seem to be headed in opposite directions. One part searches under the surface, hidden from view, doing research and development, setting up structures and finances, aiming to get the venture more rooted and secure. The other aims toward the sun and seeks to shine, to flower, wanting recognition, creating and marketing products, reaching out to spread the word and to seed new ventures. Each approach may think itself more essential.

Moly describes how these apparently rival forces, both crucial, needless to say, naturally work together in support of each other. Each takes the lead in turn; each teaches the other. The moly herb is not value-free. It synthesizes and integrates. It demands interdependence.

With moly, no man is an island.

If you dose moly you hold that perspective: like the maestro of an orchestra or a master chef, you fathom how the ingredients fit together, how they rely on each other, how they balance each other. Moly doesn't overcome or neutralize the opposites, rather it lets you work within and between them.

With moly, *you can't be enchanted* — as are Odysseus' men — by one craving or another because you see the whole picture. You won't consider hoarding as a solution. Imagine an orchestra hoarding its tuba playing. No. With moly, you get just the right amount in context.

Hermes will tell you that real wisdom does not come from a quick wit, or intelligence, or reams of hard data. People are wise when they appreciate the relationships, when they intuit the context, when they *grok* the ebb and flow of a living system. *Moly* gives that integrative perspective.

*Wisdom, we can say, is the ability to look at things from the perspective of moly.*

Jung wrote provocatively, "The ego keeps its integrity only if it does not identify with one of the opposites, and if it understands how to hold the balance between them. This is possible only if it remains conscious of both at once...Even if it were a question of some great truth, identification with it would still be a catastrophe, as it arrests all further spiritual development."[22]

## The Pen and the Sword

Circe warmly welcomes Odysseus, but when she offers him her spiked potion, he secretly protects himself with the *moly* before drinking. Circe waives her magic wand to expose Odysseus as a fat, tendentious swine, who is as greedy and enchanted as the others. Like the talented therapist that she is, she has a laser eye for what enchants her charges. She is dismayed to have no effect.

"Get thee to the pigpen," she commands.

But Odysseus raises his sword, and in this case the sword is mightier than the pen.

Circe falls to her dimpled knees; ever gorgeous, eyes wide, she looks up and blurts out, "You are enchantment-proof!" Odysseus, protected by moly, won't be enchanted. It's a good thing too, for with her adoring upward gaze, if she did not have him before, she surely would have enchanted him thus.

## Circe

Circe is probably the most celebrated sorceress in Greek myth. She attracts and guides humans and, depending on their capacity, either points them to their own greed where they get stuck, or, as we shall see, rewards them with secret wisdom and guidance about the road ahead. She explains the perils and pitfalls of the journey home, she will give you the information you need, *if you can handle the truth* without becoming enchanted.

Circe values most of all a clear head, a mind that cannot be swept away either by the emotions or the intellect, someone who is not so easily enchanted or disenchanted.

Before Odysseus meets Circe he is adrift; he has no handle on what is yet to come. After he leaves her, he has specific direction for home, a good idea of what's going to happen, and even instructions for making peace with Poseidon.

Seekers look far and wide for a guru like Circe in some exotic place, on a mountaintop or deep in the jungle; sometimes they look in a church or in a psychotherapy office.

On late night cable, "as-if" Circes abound. We see them as charlatans hawking the latest self-help seminar or selling no-money-down real estate programs. These false Circes appear to offer help, guidance for the road, but they just want you enchanted, under their spell.

How to tell the real Circe? The real Circe will always insist upon a specific course of action.

She sends Odysseus straight to Hades, to confront his unfulfilled wishes and "what might have beens."

CHAPTER SIX

# To Hades and Back
# The Death of Longing

*The dread and resistance which every human being experiences when it comes to delving too deeply into himself is, at bottom, the fear of the journey to Hades.*
— C.G. Jung

*"I see dead people… They only see what they wanna see. They don't know they're dead."*
— Cole Sear, *The Sixth Sense* (M.N. Shyamalan)

Circe explains to Odysseus that, in order to continue his journey home, he must go to Hades, the Underworld Kingdom where the departed spirits go, to consult with the famous blind oracle Tiresias who will give him further guidance.

Circe cautions him: once in Hades he will be inundated by the shades of the dead. In order to protect himself, he must dig a trench as a boundary marker, then slaughter a ram and a ewe and pour their blood into the trench. As the shades come near, all will want blood. Odysseus can choose which ones may drink. These will be able to speak; the others will fade away.

Filled with trepidation, Odysseus sails the next morning to Hades. As instructed, he digs the pit and slits the throats of the sheep over the pit, filling it with blood. He stands safely behind the trench; to do any useful work in Hades, where tempestuous emotions run high, you have to keep clear boundaries, or you will be overwhelmed.

The ghost of Tiresias materializes, knocks back his tipple of blood, and agrees to coach Odysseus.

First, he says, if Odysseus makes it to an island called Thrinacia, he will encounter some cattle sacred to Helios, the god of the Sun. Best not eat these shiny, golden cattle, warns Tiresias, or your crew will be killed and you will return to Ithaca a broken man.

Second, Tiresias instructs Odysseus that once back safely to Ithaca, Odysseus must carry his oar far inland to a race of people who know nothing of the sea until he meets a person who mistakes the oar for a fan to winnow grain. There he must plant the oar and make a sacrifice to Poseidon.

Tiresias' guidance is central to the Odyssey, and we return to it at the end.

Then, his business with Tiresias done, a large crowd of departed spirits presses close around Odysseus, each with "deep sorrow there, each asking about the grief that touched him most."

The spirit of Odysseus' mother Anticleia comes forward. Odysseus did not know she had died, and in fact she had died of a broken heart, longing for him to return. She sips the blood, she gives him what news she has of home; he makes his peace with her as best he can, and says a final farewell.

Now some dead comrades-in-arms from Troy push forward, each with an agenda, each preoccupied by his own "what-might-have-beens."

Agamemnon was bumped-off by his wife and her lover when he returned from Troy to Greece. He boils for revenge, even though he's dead.

The famed warrior Achilles bemoans his short but incredibly glorious heroic life; filled with regret, he wishes he had a long, mean and anonymous life, even as a slave to the poorest farmer, than to be a lord among the dead.

Then mighty Ajax shows his face, but he is still so fuming mad that Odysseus beat him (and maybe not so fair and square) in a footrace for the dead Achilles' armor, that he won't talk to his old friend. Ajax so identified with his humiliation by Odysseus that he took his own life. Now, he holds tight to his prideful grudge even in the Great Beyond.

Each of the shades in Hades is consumed by his own unfinished *if-onlys*, even in Hades, and even though they are dead. Haunted and immobilized by their unlived lives, they're stuck hopelessly in the past. Traumatized, they can't let go, and they can't move on.

"A trauma," writes the psychoanalyst Adam Phillips, "is whatever there is in a person's experience that resists useful redescription. Traumas, like beliefs, are ways of stopping time."[23] There is no passage of time in Hades, no recontexting of the past, no opportunity for souls to move from their old traumas into their present.

Hell, it turns out, is a place not of fire and brimstone but of something much worse: it is where we are wedded to and consumed by regrets and unfulfilled desires, jealousies, ambitions and cravings. Hades is the place of envy of the living — those who have *real lives* (and who among us has not been envious of the living?) — for their embodied experience, and of remorse for wrong life choices. These ties that bind apparently keep the dead (or the dead parts of ourselves) from moving on; they keep them in Hell. Hades is the land of what might have been, a place we are all destined to visit at one time or another.

But we all know spirits who are not merely visiting, but *stuck* in Hades, who build their entire lives around the aching sense of loss and failed dreams. They are tormented by their Big Mistake or the mean hand that Fate has dealt. Each feels, as all spirits imprisoned in Hades feel, that their own special tragedy is the worst of all, that it is unique in its accursedness, and, most wretched, that it is irredeemable.

Ajax, for his part, feels done in by heaven (since the goddess Athene, Odysseus' patroness, intervened in Odysseus' favor in that footrace), and he seems disposed to stew about it forever, labeling himself as god's victim.

Ajax demands too much of the gods to be able to move on: he demands that they be fair. Poor Ajax. He'll be stuck here a long time.

The veterans' harsh take on their own situation is more than the blues. Life has lost its color. They are all hopeless, short-changed by the world, powerless to make amends, tormented by an unhappy existence in inhospitable circumstances that appears as though it will last for eternity with No Way Out. Today we call people like this depressed.

What they lack is the virtue of equanimity, the ability to view even the tempestuous events of one's life with an evenness of mind and temper, undisturbed by agitating emotion and the pressing, unmediated attentions of specters of the psyche who will never be satisfied. What anyone needs when they visit Hades is what Circe has conceived for Odysseus in her instructions: an (emotionally) dry, safe place to stand, behind the boundary trench, where it is possible to remain cool, calm and collected in the face of turbulent feelings, and at the same time, in touch with all the shades have to tell.

These shades, vampires of the psyche, have no power over us until we give them lifeblood. If you give them too much blood — energy, focus, attention — they will suck you dry with their demands. If you give blood to the wrong spirit, you may be trapped in an emotional encounter that you do not want or need. A soulful visit to Hades depends on knowing which shades to give blood to and which to shoo away. You have to choose based not on impulse, but on implications.

However the goddess Circe shows up in our life — as a wise teacher, a therapist, a minister, a fairy godmother, a storyteller, a medicine woman, or as is more likely, without the conventional garb of a guru — her task is the same, *to give travel directions to our own personal Hades.* She guides us to discern and face honestly those places of unfulfilled longing and regret, the "if-onlys," the unlived parts of ourselves that demand to be heard. We must choose which of the clamoring spirits to give blood to — triage — and then to make our peace with them and move on.

## You'll know you're in Hades when:

- Melancholy, even depression, pervades this world.
- The local spirits are hopeless: they believe that change in their circumstances is beyond reach.
- The principal focus is on past traumas, on unfinished business, on what is lost, on what might have been.
- Little or no energy is devoted to future plans and possibilities.

## If you are in Hades

- You must decide which of your shades to give blood to and which to disregard.

- Ask your shade what story it has to tell and what insights it has to offer: Their intense story of woe and difficult feelings is likely to be true on its own terms, and it reveals where they are stuck.
- Don't counsel them to forget about the past, or that their feelings are invalid or inappropriate. If Odysseus were to tell Agamemnon to let go of his rage and to cheer up, he would seem naïve.
- Stay safe and centered behind your boundary trench. What the shades lack, and what you will need, is a safe vantage point so that you can hear their story, but are not swept away by their intense, overwhelming emotions.
- *Never give up*. Because hopelessness is central to this place, Hades is the easiest stop on the Odyssey to give up. The denizens here are the most discouraged, and feel the most like victims.
- Face honestly those shades, unlived or unfinished parts of yourself, make peace with them and go on.

CHAPTER SEVEN

# The Sirens
# Killing Me Softly

By following Circe's clear guidance, Odysseus has been able to listen to the voices of despair in Hades, the unfinished ghosts of his past, while protected safely from behind his boundary trench, so that these spirits do not overwhelm him. Though many thirsty spirits vie for his attention, it's up to him (as it is for each of us) to assess which spectres he will draw to him and give lifeblood to, and which he will ignore. Here is a man, Odysseus, who now can choose life, not perfunctorily like most, but mindfully, because he has experienced the dead parts of himself. When he sails back from death to the light he is reborn.

*Except a man be born again,*
*he cannot see the Kingdom of God.*
— JOHN 3:3

After leaving Circe's care, and per her prediction, Odysseus passes the Sirens' Island. The Sirens are the notorious temptresses of travelers. Half-woman and half-bird, they sing exquisitely to seduce passing travelers to scuttle their boats on the rocky point. The Sirens' beach is littered with the rotting bones of previous travelers who did not make it past.

Circe has forewarned Odysseus to stuff his sailors' ears with wax so that they cannot hear the poignant song; Odysseus may listen, she says, but he must have his men bind him tightly to the mast so that he will not scuttle the boat.

As his ship sails past the Sirens, Odysseus listens and immediately realizes that they are playing his song.

Saint Ambrose thought that the Sirens represented worldly desires and that the ship's mast stood for Christ's cross; the moral of the story then would be that the advertent Christian should tie himself to the cross when tempted by the Sirens' song. But then why does Circe, who proposes that Odysseus arrange to be tied up, say it's OK to listen to the Sirens at all? Other commentators have said that the Sirens' song is really the offer of success or fame or riches, but it is much more seductive than that.

The Sirens sing:

*"Come here," they sang, "legendary Odysseus*
*And listen to our voices*
*No one ever sailed by without staying for our song*
*We know all the ills that the gods*
*laid upon [the Greeks] and the Trojans*
*And we can tell you everything that is going*
*to happen from those wars."*[24]

The Sirens' song is "I feel your pain." The Sirens promise understanding of your most private anguish. What song could be sweeter? And then they promise to let you know if there is any meaning to your struggles, any hope for the future. *Who wouldn't die to listen?*

Circe says Odysseus can listen to the Sirens' song, because not to listen is to cut oneself off from a profound longing — to have one's private pain acknowledged — and from a profound hope — that it may turn out all right, that it was all worthwhile.

We know people who travel determinedly through life, rowing hard, but their ears are stuffed with wax so that they won't be distracted by the Sirens' song; they have given up the prospect that the ache in their heart can be known and understood, and they have given up the search for their life's meaning. What a parched existence: they miss the lovesome pleasure that comes when someone sings to them that their voyage is known and appreciated, and, without having heard the Sirens' song, they won't be able to sing it for someone else. They are cut off indeed.

But here is Circe's most important *caveat*: Odysseus may be seduced by the wonderful sound of the Sirens, but he cannot be consumed by it. He cannot act upon it*; he cannot orient his course toward the Sirens,* or he will be destroyed, as it is with every traveler. Those who are distracted from their journey home to focus on the sound of their own unique pain, who are consumed by exploring it, how sad and beautiful it is, driven to understand it with endless therapies and explorations, and to make others understand — "Why me? Why this? Why now?" — risk devastation on the Sirens' rocks.

Now Odysseus moves from lands of deeply personal emotional exploration, Hades and the Sirens' island, to an adventure which is practical and worldly. Here Odysseus will be judged strictly by his results, and not how artfully he explores the depth of his feelings.

CHAPTER EIGHT

# Scylla and Charybdis
# Necessary Losses

Circe has warned Odysseus of a dire strait through which he will pass on his way home. On one side atop a rocky crag is the grisly monster Scylla, who has six heads, each with a mouth sporting a triple row of fangs. Just opposite Scylla — "an arrow shot apart" and underwater — is the monster Charybdis, who three times a day gulps a colossal deluge of sea water to churn a terrifying whirlpool.

Circe tells Odysseus that he will *inevitably* lose six men, one to each of Scylla's heads, but nevertheless to "stay hard by Scylla's rock and sail past her as fast as you can! It's better to lose the six men, than lose your whole crew and ship" to Charybdis' whirlpool.

But Odysseus is not happy. He wants to avoid Charybdis, certainly, but still fight Scylla. He doesn't want to lose *any* men. "So stubborn!" says Circe. Get over yourself, she advises.

You can't fight Scylla. Scylla will scarf up her six sailors by their heads no matter what. (Scylla takes her share off the top.) That's the way it is. Let her have her due, says Circe, then flee. If you try to fight off the monster, Circe warns, Scylla will take more men. Why fight battles you can't win, ego-boy?

Charybdis, the whirlpool maker, is the opposite alternative: if you come too close, you get flooded, overwhelmed, inundated, sucked under. All is lost.

Being "between Scylla and Charybdis" — the original rock and a hard place — has come to mean being stuck "between two equally hazardous alternatives."[25] For George Sandys, who curiously was the first treasurer of the Jamestown colony, Virginia, writing in 1632, "The dangerous sailing between Scylla and Charybdis commends the safetie of the Middle Course, and deterres from either extremetie."[26]

But Homer's meaning is more subtle and more pointed. For Homer, these monsters appear when — in order to reach a clear, practical goal (getting through the straits) — you are obliged to take necessary losses (Scylla) to avoid complete devastation (Charybdis).

When between two inescapable monsters, the only sensible course is to take those unavoidable losses and keep moving. "Just do it," Circe says.

Her advice is not meant to be desperate, quite the contrary. When you know how the devils work, when you understand the rhythms of even a difficult situation, you have the opportunity for hope, not despair.

Odysseus must be efficient and consistent — he must execute well, sail well — but he must keep his ego in check and not get caught in a futile, vain, self-indulgent effort to deny Scylla her due or to take revenge. This is not the time to be imaginative or clever, or to think outside the box. This is the time to stay on task, goal in mind, with pride and ego stowed away. Getting through counts as a win. It's the simple, sleek workaday solution that succeeds here.

Here you are judged not on your history or your pedigree, but how you perform. This is the time for discipline and focus on the main purpose at hand. And at this Odysseus excels.

Speed is essential (if you dawdle, Scylla will have a second helping) and so is efficiency, but you must also be tactical. If you rush blindly and breathlessly toward your goal, you'll end up in Charybdis' tank.

People who do well between Scylla and Charybdis are oriented toward results: they keep the goal in mind and are willing to be judged by their outcomes. Inevitably they are motivated by achievement, productivity and success.

They must have a taste for practical action, too: they need to be good at moving around obstacles, at parrying problems, at adjusting to what the boss or the market or the customer requires.

Scylla and Charybdis appear in fast moving operations like a brokerage or sales outfit, where new opportunities come and keep coming. The day is filled with many small losses, Scylla taking her due, but there is little time for regret. If you try to prevent inevitable losses, if you try to bat a thousand, if you get stuck in your vanity, if you try to avenge each affront, Scylla eats more men. You need to keep moving, Circe says.

If you head across the strait and hug close to the whirlpool in order to avoid any losses to Scylla, you're open to the greedy Charybdic mistakes: big picture or large systems failures, Enron-class goofs, that overwhelm the operation and shut it down. When a brokerage bets the firm on an undiversified large holding with the idea of avoiding *any* small losses, they invite disaster. Charybdic mistakes must be avoided at all costs.

Odysseus is past master of finagling, cutting corners, dissembling, and general smooth-talking, fast-walking manipulation. Just ask the Cyclops. But Scylla and Charybdis are not interested in his jive. They are a hard-nosed reality check, a call to honesty within oneself. There is no conning them and no negotiation. Here, the feedback is fast and furious and the results are everything. A "strait forward" attitude gets you through. There is no magic here and the gods will not intervene. With no opportunity for his usual con games, Odysseus has a hard lesson to learn.

Nor is there time in the straits of Scylla and Charybdis for psychologizing, for reframing, or for philosophical or technical complexity. Simple, frequent, concrete feedback about clearly defined goals is what the situation demands. The question *here* is never, "How can I do this perfectly?" The question is always: What is good enough to get the job done?

**You'll know you're between Scylla and Charybdis when:**

- You must balance between niggling losses and complete devastation in a fast-moving environment.
- The emphasis is on efficiency and effectiveness, on results and the bottom line.
- Choices and decisions come and keep coming. Feedback is frequent and direct.
- The parameters for success are clear. You are judged on whether you get the job done.

**If you're between Scylla and Charybdis:**

- Know what the goals are, what counts as a win.
- Stay flexible regarding tactics — you may have to adjust your plan as you go.
- Just do it. That's what matters here.
- Keep moving. If you dawdle, Scylla will have a second helping.
- Take the necessary losses and move on. Scylla will take her due no matter what. It is the cost of doing business.

CHAPTER NINE

# The Cattle of the Sun
# Going for the Gold

*Real successful people have to cut corners and manipulate. That's the way things get done.*
— JOHN Z. DE LOREAN

*Gold is the sun; to make gold is to become God.*
— VICTOR HUGO, *NOTRE-DAME DE PARIS*

Odysseus and his crew next head toward the Island of Thrinacia, home to a herd of precious golden cattle that belong to the Sun god, Helios. Both Circe and Tiresias have warned Odysseus not to eat these sacred cows because Helios will take serious revenge. "Don't even go there," Circe has told him, "you have to respect the gods."

But the tired and peckish crew insists on landing, so Odysseus makes the crew swear an oath that they will not eat the cattle. Alas, once on the island the men are stranded by the blustery weather. Eventually the food from Circe runs out, which is to say her nourishing guidance, and when Odysseus goes inland to pray to the gods, the men panic that they will go hungry. Fearing a painful death by starvation, they break their oath and slaughter the best of the golden cattle.

But the cattle meat writhes and actually moans ominously on the roasting spit, not a good sign.

As the crew prepares the barbeque, Eurylochus proposes, "Why, when we're back in Ithaca we'll build a beautiful temple to the sun god and throw in plenty of gifts to make up for our sin!" Like some dodgy businessman, or some college student about to cheat on a test, he *rationalizes*, "Well, I have to lie or cheat now to make it through, that's the way the system works. Everybody does it, but I'll make it right later on."

Eurylochus hopes the end will justify the means. But when your crew presumes to decide for the god what will appease him, you know they are in super-deep trouble.

Eurylochus is preaching *hubris,* plain and simple, the sin of defying the gods (ME, *defy*, "to renounce faith in"). The choice of whether the cattle should live or die is, by natural law, solely the sun god's. Odysseus' crew take for themselves the sun god's rights and privileges; they make themselves into false gods with great powers. They pretend to be people they are not.

When Helios hears the news of the slaughter of his precious cattle, he is, not surprisingly, incensed. He demands satisfaction from Zeus, or he threatens rudely, crudely, to shine where the sun don't shine: in Hades (that is, to turn the world upside down.) "No, no," says Zeus. "Don't do that. You will have your revenge."

When the strong winds finally ease up on Thrinacia, Odysseus and the crew set sail. And true to his word, Zeus mounts a terrible storm, bombarding Odysseus' ship with his signature lightning and thunder, scuttling the ship. All hands are lost except for Odysseus, who survives by clinging to the mast.

In the Bible, when Moses ascended Mount Sinai but did not return when expected, the Israelites mint a false god from their own jewelry, the infamous golden calf. They worship their false god, as so many of us do with money or fame or accomplishment, hoping — much as Odysseus' men — that it would nourish and comfort them in their hour of darkness and confusion.

Instead, the Israelites' idolatry nearly gets them annihilated by a jealous G-d who insists on justice for violation of His laws; G-d smites some 3000 of the blasphemers and condemns the remainder to wander the desert until they die; none of this generation will be allowed to enter the Promised Land; none of them will be allowed home. None will become their real self. Why so harsh a punishment for travelers just trying to survive?

Indeed, Odysseus' men are destroyed by Zeus, with a punishment as harsh as the Hebrews suffered in the Sinai desert, and for the same reason: for their blasphemy — creating and worshipping false gods — these Ithacans won't be allowed to make it home either.

What's so universally unpardonable about putting your faith in golden cattle?

From the point of view of the psyche, false gods, golden cattle and sacred cows are held in the *persona.* The *persona* (Gr. "mask") is the face that we present to the world, our social ambitions. Jung called the persona the false self, the person we are pretending to be, the way we want to be perceived and are perceived. The comedian Billy Crystal emphasized the importance of the persona when he opined, "It's better to look good than to feel good."

The persona struts an *idealized image* — more together, smarter, more successful, more compassionate, a few inches taller perhaps, than we are — pretending to others (and more problematically to oneself) that this façade is the real you. Personas vary from person to person. A person packages his persona according to the way he imagines it should look in the context of a specific situation or set of circumstances. The valued image may rely on beauty or power or intelligence or godliness or some other quality. (Looking good on Main Street is different than success on Jump Street.) Most people will have little trouble telling you the way they hope to be perceived.

Jung comments with particular world-wisdom, "One could say, with little exaggeration, that the persona is that which in reality one is not, but which oneself as well as others think one is. In any case, the temptation to be what one seems to be is great, because the persona is usually rewarded in cash."[27] The persona, the home of your false gods, is the place where you sell yourself instead of being yourself.

Playing a grand role, or taking up the qualities of a hero, can be great fun, an imaginative "trying on" of archetypes, as when children pretend to be invulnerable action stars, or when avid football fans identify with their home team's unlikely comeback, or when persons named Goldberg associate themselves with the brilliant, champion wrestler named Goldberg. If the image is playful, inspires one to possibilities, deepens self-discovery, then it can be enlivening.

But by slaughtering and eating the golden cattle, Odysseus' men don't simply role-play the sun god: they claim his rights and privileges for themselves. *They try to take his place.* As psychoanalyst Karen Horney points out, believing one is one's persona makes one *arrogant*, in the original sense of the word: one arrogates to oneself powers and abilities that one does not have.

The Israelites are in the same quandary: they try to replace their real G-d with a false god made from their own ornaments, as it happens. But the false (self-made) god does not nourish, and the real G-d will want satisfaction. From the point of view of the psyche, when the shiny, counterfeit persona is substituted for the real self, we have a sure recipe for disaster.

Odysseus faces quite a few calamities, but the failure in Thrinacia — insisting that your persona, your false god, save you — is the *only certain route* to catastrophe on this Odyssey. If you decide to become your inauthentic self, how can you make it home, the place where you are most who you really are?

Now, for the first time since his Odyssey began, Odysseus is alone. He's lost all his crew. He's lost his ship and his prospects are bleak. After nine days adrift, naked as the day he was born, he washes up on the shores of the island of Ogygia, home to the goddess Calypso.

CHAPTER TEN

# Calypso Animation

*"Don't eat at places called Mom's"*

Barely clinging to a scrap of wood from his ship, exhausted and with no likely prospects, Odysseus drifts on the sea for nine days until he washes up on the Island of Ogygia, the exquisite home of Calypso, a goddess who offers more comfort and succor than it is possible to imagine.

Calypso's sumptuous, impossibly lush island is a compelling paradise. Cypress and poplar trees abound, fragrant cedar and juniper wood burns in the fireplaces, grapes grow wild, the violets and parsley are in bloom. Splendor is in the grass.

And the stunning, elegantly feminine Calypso takes Odysseus to her meticulous custody. She dresses him like a god, she cooks him mouth-watering delicacies, she nurses him back to health from the brink of death; her nymphs massage his sore feet and attend to his every possibility but one: Calypso herself insists on sharing her divine bed.

Calypso's island Ogygia is the out-of-the-way place where we go, alone and travel-weary, to be taken care of, to be nurtured, to heal.

Shangri-La, from the novel by James Hilton, is such a place. Shangri-La is a hard-to-find lamasery in the Himalayas, and is much like Ogygia: remote but sunny, lushly fertile, indescribably idyllic. Should you find your way there — always after a long and difficult trip — the High Lama can indulge all your personal desires: for wisdom or lucre and even for love. And in Shangri-La you don't grow old (much like Calypso's forthcoming offer of immortality to Odysseus). But if you leave, the beneficence is petulantly cancelled. The High Lama, like Calypso, meets your needs as long as you're willing to be completely dependent on him.

And therein lies the rub.

Calypso is the archetypal nurturer with the personal touch: she gratifies your wishes — these are *your* wishes, the ones personal to you — as you barely can imagine them. She pampers, flatters and encourages. She is attentive and caring. There is no denying that Calypso at her best dispenses sensuous pleasures and soulful healing.

But serious strings attach. Under the guise of helping, she demands to be in tight control of Odysseus and of his world.

She says in effect, like some overbearing nurse in a hospital, or like a government benefits clerk who signs the checks and holds all the cards, "I am only here to help you. Therefore you have to do everything my way."

She will grant all his desires except the only one that counts: He cannot return to Penelope and to real life. She asks that Odysseus give up his precious journey home in return for her considerable favors.

But, by the time we meet Odysseus, we see that Calypso's burdensome attentions, however pleasurable they may have been, are now empty: they humiliate and imprison more than they nourish. She is his lover, and she is his jailor, too.

*"Blessed are those who weep."*
— MATTHEW 5:4

So, after seven long years with Calypso, we find Odysseus on a rocky promontory by the sea. He is inconsolable. He aches for home and his real life, but he has got himself stuck here. He is ashamed of himself. He has sold himself out, and for a poor price.

But even so, each day he continues to indulge his perquisites, the sensuous massages, the delicious food and the creature comforts. And yes, he still lies with Calypso every night; and it is most certainly a lie because he has Penelope on his mind.

(Later he says he felt *obliged* to be intimate with Calypso, but that takes guest etiquette to a new level.)

He has put aside the deeply sensible person he knows himself to be for these hollow pleasures which do not nurture him. Each day he is shamed by the disparity between who he is — great king and warrior and soul mate to magnificent Penelope, beloved by Athene herself (and so powerfully annoying as to be personally despised by Poseidon himself) — and who he has become: a low-rent gigolo for a minor goddess who lives way out in the sticks.

We are humiliated with him, for him. What has become of the great Odysseus? He has hit bottom. He is utterly pathetic.

For a long while at Calypso's he has tried to override his guilt, to hide from himself behind appearances and amusements (Gr, *kalypto*, to hide; *apo-calypse*, revelation); but now he sinks into his self-pity, wallows in it, is ready to drown in it. And this will be his salvation. Ultimately his self-pity will draw him back into life. The psychologist James Hillman writes, "Self-pity is the beginning of caring deeply about oneself...For self-pity is a form of self-discovery, self-revelation; it reveals my longings to myself. What really matters to my deepest, most vulnerable and touchy part is revealed."[28]

**Anima**

In the world of the psyche, Calypso is an archetype of the inner feminine, which Jung called the *anima*. The anima, he wrote, is "the glamorous, possessive, moody and sentimental seductress."[29] She is a traveler's link to the juicy pleasure in being alive, to the savory appetite for one's destiny, to creativity and inspiration. She is, or can be, an inordinately powerful guide to what is really important in a person's life.

When the relationship goes well, she draws one into life. Without a good relationship with his anima, Jung said, a man is bereft of "erotic longing."[30]

Calypso appears in the outer world as the adoring wife or girlfriend, the doting mother, the heartening colleague or solicitous employee, the therapist with delicious chicken soup, all of whom flatter with *customized,* hyper-intense, laser-focused *personal* attentions.[31]

Calypso can appear as an organization as well, where appreciating and doing good through one-on-one relationships is central, perhaps a community mental health agency or a business that focuses on legendary, individualized, customer service or advice: think Nordstrom or Mary Kay cosmetics.

Her possibilities are grand. For those who need to be organized, she can manage a person's life. For those who are lonely, she can provide a *prêt-a-porter* social life. She can pacify the anxious and build the egos of those who doubt themselves. She delivers emotional supplies for the traveler, just what is needed, when they are needed and exactly the way the traveler likes them served up. She is, as Jung said of the anima, "the solace for all the bitterness of life."[32]

A person may become too independent of the anima. If a traveler shuts out her *élan vital* and her sweet help, the traveler may well become world weary, crusty and rigid, a sourpuss. Such a traveler may have given up on the hope that life could be nourishing.

But if on the other hand, a person is seduced by the anima — with her gifts and attentions she promises that she will make a luscious life for the traveler if only she can run things, if only the traveler will give up the silly journey to Ithaca — it is fair to say that the traveler is lost, marooned on Calypso's island.

We've all met travelers snatched by Calypso. Ogygia is more than comfy, at least at first.

But then we see that, like our hero, a person gets locked into apparent pleasures — a job or a partner or a house or a life — that he or she imagined would nurture one's soul but then do not. Instead they diminish the traveler, who has sold out the journey home.

So many travelers, who are *so close*, just a penultimate stop from home like Odysseus, get bogged down, addicted to Calypso's empty pleasures and they don't realize that their central problem is that they have forgotten *how to value.*

Without realizing it, the traveler stuck in dependency at Calypso's has lost the ability to head for home, having forgotten what is really worthwhile in life; he or she has forgotten how to value for oneself, including most especially, to value oneself, to be in touch with one's own true worth. The traveler has forgotten what callings resonate with his or her soul. A person can spend years or a lifetime, just like Odysseus, possessed by the anima, moping around, frantically trying to find some self-worth in Calypso's considerable but hollow pleasures.

Calypso sometimes takes a bad rap for being so demanding, but she performs a crucial service, by design or not. She kills Odysseus' ego by drowning it in its own desires. *She insists, by flooding him with the inessential, the superficial, the seductive, that he distinguish between what is essential and what is false in his life.*

The experience of Calypso makes a traveler crave his real home.

## "Immortality? I'd die first."

Calypso tries to keep Odysseus right where he is. She unveils her ultimate seduction: she proposes to make Odysseus immortal if he will stay with her.

Odysseus has the opportunity to live forever in a never-ending fool's paradise; it is an elegant life of leisure, to be fed, housed, clothed and taken care of, with no money worries. The only catch is that he would give up the possibility of home. This is a startling offer, and many travelers will make the deal. (Consider those poor souls who marry into great wealth but then make nothing of their lives.)

Unfortunately, for all the advantages of immortality, someone who cannot really die cannot really live. (The gods are immortal, but for all their cosmic *Sturm und Drang*, their scuffles don't matter so much to them. They keep their dominions and generally go on as before. Little is really at stake.)

So Odysseus turns Calypso down cold; he chooses to live the life of a mortal man. It is an extraordinary choice, a seminal choice. It is the only way he can be a hero. How many of us would so choose?

Immortality is death to humans. Odysseus' audacious choice to be mortal makes his life meaningful.

**Athene**

Now Odysseus' tears of shame reach Mount Olympus, to his champion the goddess Athene. From on high, Athene looks down at her beloved protégé and she sees that he has suffered enough.

Athene was born full-bore from the head of Zeus, which makes her the expression of celestial good sense. She sees the world as it is. She knows how to think clearly. *She knows how to value.* Her famous attribute is *metis*, the shrewd, *practical*, strategic intelligence (street smarts) which is also Odysseus' specialty, but which he has somehow misplaced while he has been captivated by Calypso.

At the council on Olympus, Athene makes her case to her father Zeus, arguing with pristine, objective *logic* for fairness: Odysseus has been too long delayed, she says; he has learned his lessons and needs to get on with his destiny, and he needs to get home. As a matter of principle, she argues, the gods owe protection to those like Odysseus who have offered the proper respect. "He was made for more than this," she says in effect.

Who wouldn't want the goddess Athene as an advocate before Olympus, demanding justice, pointing out to the gods that he or she has suffered enough, insisting that promises of Ithaca made long ago be kept? But how to connect with Athene?

We know the arguments she favors: Clear thinking Athene has a practical, logical bent. "Think clearly, " she says. "Think practically." When the TV psychologist Dr. Phil says "Get real," he is invoking Athene.

When a traveler finally can see this real-world situation clearly — neither drowning in self-pity, a victim (too dependent and shamed), nor trying to pull himself up by the bootstraps without the help of Heaven (too independent and prideful) — that is when Athene is invoked. Athene appears at the decisive moment, ready to distinguish real from false, what is worthwhile from what is not.

Athene, mistress of strategy, makes the right move at the right time: With Odysseus' nemesis Poseidon away on a business trip to Ethiopia, Zeus agrees with his daughter Athene. Nobody can cut through red tape like Zeus: after all this time, Odysseus will be Ithaca in a matter of days.

Zeus sends his herald Hermes to serve a writ of *habeas corpus*. Calypso must free Odysseus at once.

Calypso reluctantly, resentfully submits to Zeus' order, as of course she must. Now it is her turn to play the victim, to act the martyr. "How can the gods do this to me? To *me?*," she explodes.

It's not only Odysseus who has trouble finding his self-worth in this dreamy, gooey, faraway place. Although she is too proud to admit it, Calypso too, desperately searches for her own value in her relationship with Odysseus. Can she somehow use her wiles and her powers to control him and keep him prisoner, dependent upon her, and thereby (she imagines) enhance her own self-concept?

Calypso is, in the modern word, codependent: she finds her worth in being needed by another. Calypso tries so hard to please Odysseus, and in return for her attentiveness and her magnificent gifts, *expects* to be appreciated and depended upon and perhaps even loved. When her efforts do not bring the desired results, she ends up indignant with Zeus and all the gods.

But then something magical: When Zeus frees Odysseus, Calypso is also freed from her codependent drama. With no strings attached, we now see Calypso, a natural helper, at her best.

Calypso agrees to advise and supply Odysseus for the trip. She gives Odysseus a great two-handed ax, custom-fitted to his palms (she is the princess of the personal touch) to fell trees, and an adze so he can fashion a raft, which he does with great pleasure and consummate skill. Calypso also supplies sail cloth and prepares bread and wine and clothes for his journey.

If a traveler has a good give-and-take with the anima — neither letting her run things nor ignoring her gifts (neither too dependent or independent) — she can do the serious work of bringing a traveler into real life.

If a traveler knows and trusts what has personal significance, he or she cannot get mired in Calypso's pleasures; Calypso won't be able to take over and make the big decisions. If a traveler is able to feel into what is personally important, without believing that he or she has to sell out to get it, Calypso can't muddy the waters with false needs.

Instead she becomes our finest collaborator and guide. Odysseus must design and build his own raft, but Calypso expertly helps him help himself.

Now, for the first time in a long, long time, Odysseus has hope for the future. Calypso has rekindled his spirit. He is *re-animated.* He sails on to meet his destiny.

## You'll know you're in Ogygia because:

- Ogygia is magical and delicious, just what you wanted and hoped for, at least at first.
- Calypso's seductions and services will be especially customized for and brilliantly targeted at *you personally.*
- In return, Calypso demands that you be dependent upon her, and she insists on being adored and appreciated for all she does for you.
- Her flattery and her gifts, while attractive, do not ultimately nourish. Ogygia is a pale reflection of home.

## If you are in Ogygia

- Ogygia is the place to clarify what really matters: what is your true calling? And what seemed essential but really doesn't matter at all?

- Calypso can claim power only in those areas where you agree to be dependent upon her: For what dodgy boon will you sell out Penelope and your real self?
- Keep fierce Athene's *metis* (practical wisdom) in mind. When Athene sees someone who is under her aegis swept away by a frivolous emotional adventure, the goddess may give a smack upside the head so that her mentee will say, "*Damn*, what *was* I thinking?" Your own relationship with Athene keeps you clear-headed and sensible. It is your principal insurance against being marooned permanently on Calypso's island.
- Speak from your real needs without demand or apology. Calypso responds masterfully to need and has the expertise to heal the deep wounds that come from traveling, to supply necessities for the road ahead, and to rekindle one's spirit, if she is so inclined.
- Thank her very much. Calypso likes to be thanked. Be as specific as you can be. Proud Calypso appreciates appreciation and gratitude.

NOTE: Sometimes Circe and Calypso are thrown together as matching sorceresses, and indeed they share the capacity to be both dangerous and helpful. Both beautiful goddesses mesmerize Odysseus with their charms and their enchanting islands. They are both intimate with the great man, and they serve him delicious meals and offer essential guidance, but they are opposite in their significance.

Circe, who is detached and cool, gives Odysseus travel directions to Hades. She teaches him how to separate himself from his life, *how to die*. She teaches him to come to terms with the shades who haunt him with unfinished business. She teaches him how to let go and move on.

On the other hand, Calypso, who is intense and engaged, seduces Odysseus back into life with her pleasures. She teaches him *how to live;* she leaves him with the certain knowledge that his *connectedness* to home and Penelope are most important in his heart.

CHAPTER ELEVEN

# The Phaecians Do the Right Thing

Some people stay in Calypso's womb forever, struggling with the issues of their own independence. But now Odysseus moves from the playing field of his own feelings to a larger life, to concern with virtue and its expression in community.

Odysseus' nemesis Poseidon, on his way back to Olympus from his visit with the Ethiopians, spies Odysseus on his raft at sea. Still nursing his endless, unappeasable grudge, Poseidon conceives a massive tidal wave inundating Odysseus and swamping the raft.

The sodden, bedraggled Odysseus is washed ashore on Scheria, island home to the high-minded Phaecians. These people are brilliant seafarers with the extraordinary ability to sail anywhere on earth and back within one day (the original day cruise).

Odysseus awakes on a riverbank, where he is discovered by the sumptuously sweet, young maiden Nausicaa, who is princess of the realm. Odysseus senses, correctly, that it's extremely important to mind his manners in this place; he speaks to the refined

Nausicaa gently, with restraint and courtesy and modesty (and indeed these are particular virtues of the Phaecians).

Princess Nausicaa offers him soap for washing and oil for anointing, and, thanks to a quick makeover by Athene, he emerges from the bath transformed, glowing, godlike. Nausicaa invites him to follow her wagon toward town so that he can meet the king and queen, but she suggests demurely, for the sake of propriety, that once they reach the outskirts of the walled city Odysseus should make his own way to the palace. In Scheria, appearances matter and people will talk.

At the palace, Odysseus pleads on bended knee with King Alcinoos and Queen Arete to grant him passage home. Since the naturally benevolent Phaecians see it as their duty to be gracious to travelers — duty is their bottom line — they promise to sail the following day, after a festival of epic songs and Olympic contests. "You will still have to live out your life that the gods have ordained," Alcinoos tells Odysseus, but at least he will be home.

The next day at the festival, Odysseus, who still has not said who he is, requests of the house singer-songwriter Demodocus, that he sing a song about the famous escapade of the Trojan Horse, which just happens to have been Odysseus' most renowned war exploit. Luckily, Demodocus has Odysseus' story in his repertoire.

Odysseus is deeply moved; he realizes that even after his long years of wandering, even though he has been so utterly lost and isolated, incommunicado with real life, knocked around by various thugs, not so well supported by his team, confused about what was important, and unable to shake off the curses that haunt him — in spite of all of it — his story is nevertheless known and sung by this elegant community. He covers his face and sobs into his cape.

And then the contests begin:

*Let us proceed therefore to the athletic sports,*
*So that our guest on his return home*
*may be able to tell his friends*
*How much we surpass all other nations*
*As boxers, wrestlers, jumpers, and runners.*[33]

Odysseus at first refuses to participate in these games — he really just wants a lift home and doesn't want to fool around at sports. He says with a twinge of self-pity, "I've suffered so much. Don't mind me. I'll just wait here until you're done." But the Phaecian Broadsea (Euryalos) *goads* him: "You really don't have the talents to compete." It *works*. Odysseus responds, "Why you little sonofa....you make my blood boil!"

At first Broadsea seems gauche, out of line, but then we understand: the Phaecian's grace is to spur folks to show their special talents. Even their gaming betrays a higher purpose.

Odysseus wows all with a monster discus throw; he offers to take on all comers in boxing, wrestling and foot racing. Now he's on fire, full of his powers; he wants to show what he can do.

But Odysseus catches himself: he worries that he might seem bigheaded. King Alcinoos tells him not to worry (and gives him a big clue about why he is here): "You're not bad-mannered. You just want to show your god-given talents."

## Virtue

*"Your light must shine before people,*
*so that they will see*
*the good things that you do."*
— Matthew, 5:16

The calling of the Phaecians, who are the ideal of the gracious community, is to encourage you to show your natural gifts and to provide a playing field for same. These gifts have been known since the oldest times as your virtues, your natural powers, the expression of the essential self. ("Arete," which is the Phaecian Queen's name, means "virtue" or "excellence" in the sense of "being the best you can be.")

Plato and his school believed that each of us is born with our virtues, that they become corrupted by the compromises we make with the world as it is, and that our task is to allow them natural expression. Virtues are our powers that allow us to know ourselves and overcome dangers and distractions along the way: Plato named temperance, wisdom, courage and justice; medieval Christians added faith, hope and charity.

For Plato, expression of the virtues was key to the health and harmony of the soul. Without exercising your virtues, you can't make it home. That's why the Phaecians goad Odysseus to participate in their community Olympics. The Phaecians know the virtues must be exercised and tested to be of any good. What good is it to be good only in theory?

When someone complains that their life has lost its significance, and that they are alienated or disconnected or depressed, likely they have lost touch with the expression of their virtues, "the gifts they were born with," their very particular, personal abilities to act with prerogative in the world.

## The Phaecians

When my father first read the Odyssey to me, I was a young boy and the Phaecians interested me least. No wonder. They are disciplined and proper, orderly and conventional. These were not the virtues of my youth.

The Phaecians are exquisitely *senex* (*Lt,* "old man"); they have the values of a grown-up. They are people of integrity and steadiness; they are generous, self-sacrificing and wise. Unlike gushy, emotionally labile Calypso, they are restrained and self-possessed. They hold strong views of how a civilized adult should be (gracious and dutiful), and the way a conflict should be resolved (with good will, with deliberation, based on principles), and the way a house should look (elegant and orderly).

They are courteous, concerned with etiquette and the comfort of their guest. Unlike their cousins the Cyclopes, for example, they honor the gods and they are excellent hosts to strangers.

Phaeacia is Utopia. King Alicnoos' castle is architectural perfection. He has a perfect garden where the fruit trees — pear, pomegranate and apple — serve up perfectly ripe fruit all year long, and there is always enough.

The Phaecians are expert sailors with the very highest standards: they never go off course, they never make mistakes. They are the total quality managers of their day who focus on best practices.

But most of all they are concerned with their *duty*.

For each event or experience, they consciously, thoughtfully consider "What is our duty? What is the right thing to do? What is the ideal way to proceed?"

And then they try to do it.

After a palace discussion, the Phaecians decide to grant Odysseus passage, not for money or fame, or even out of compassion, and not because some god has urged them, but because it is the right thing to do. For them, Odysseus' plea for help presents a purely *ethical* question: What is our responsibility to this man? The Phaecians are the ultimate *menschen*.

They will judge themselves — and without question these finicky people *will* judge themselves — on whether they in fact return Odysseus to Ithaca and not whether they meant well or they tried their best.

Even the risk of angering a god does not faze the Phaecians; like Hebrew National, they have to answer to *a higher authority* than even the Olympians: their sense of duty and honor. More than any beings he meets on his long Odyssey, the Phaecians have a moral dimension; they know that they are part of an undertaking that is larger than themselves.

Now gently and respectfully, King Alcinous asks Odysseus for his name and his story.

The critical event at Scheria, and central in his return, is that Odysseus tells his story. Of course if he did not tell it, you likely would not be reading it. But in a deeper sense, the most profound learnings of the Odyssey are tied to the virtues of telling one's story.

## Story: The Call to Account

*It's hard for me to tell all this like a god.*
— HOMER, *ILIAD* 12:176

*In every era, God calls to every man:*
*"Where are you in your world? So many years*
*and days of those allotted to you have passed,*
*and how far have you gotten in your world?"*
—MARTIN BUBER, *TALES OF THE HASIDIM*

The Phaecians ask for Odysseus' story (Gr. *mythos*) and by so asking invite him to account for himself. The call to account is very high. You hear it when someone asks, "What's your story? Where have you been and where do you propose to go?"

Odysseus takes the question seriously. He tells his adventures, where he has succeeded and how he has failed, the lessons he has learned, and where he has been virtuous and where he has been clueless.

When Odysseus tells his story, he is recognized for who he is, a truly remarkable man. The Phaecians can recognize him, not from the way he looks or dresses, but because they now know his story.

There is no way to understand our life, let alone the life of another — what is good and what is off the mark, what are the acts of a hero and what are the acts of a *schlemiel* — except through the telling of our story. You need the context. The Phaecians, the mavens of virtue, teach that by telling our story we can discern our true virtues, and also how the circumstances of our failures and frustrations may hold significance.

The story can and does change, and so does our hero. Odysseus at the Cyclops', smug and demanding, is very different than the perfectly humble houseguest who visits the Phaecians. Odysseus' context changes every time he takes a sea cruise. Those travelers whose framework does not change are surely stuck in a single episode of their own odyssey.

When we cannot tell a story about our odyssey that holds meaning for the teller — a story that answers the question "why give a hoot?" — we move towards alienation, towards all kinds of desperation, maybe even depression or worse. If you don't know what story you are weaving, how can you choose one thing over another? How can you know what values are crucial? How can you know where you have been *bona fide* and where you have missed the mark? How can you know, as we asked at the start, what is meaningful and what is not? Most of all, how can you find home?

Odysseus' story — according to the first lines of *The Odyssey* — is the story of a man of many turns who, on his way home, comes to know the minds of many men and becomes skilled in all ways of contending. A traveler, he takes his journey personally: there can be no doubt that it has meaning for him and for others.

And so each traveler must find *a place*, "someplace where everybody knows your name" as the song has it, *to tell the story* of our adventures, to live the meaning of our journey and to be called to account: it is most often the place where you are in community, where people want *you* to show your virtues, *demand* that you show your virtues.

The arrival at the community of the Phaecians means you are at a point where your hero's story — the story of this journey — is ready to be told and heard. It's the necessary stop right before home.

The Phaecians, grown-ups, are the key to the grown-up inner life. The Phaecians speak numinously of our need to do our duty, which said another way is our need to belong — to see and be seen — to have real roots and a real home. So that while one's odyssey is about transformation — about ripening knowledge into wisdom and growing talents into virtues — it is also, actually and practically, about making one's way home.

Martha Stewart, the sometime embattled domestic goddess, is a Phaecian; she, too, is an expert on matters horticultural and culinary; she is fussy, adamant about details, and concerned about etiquette, flawless entertaining and living the good life; but most of all, like the Phaecians, she is obsessive about figuring the best way to do "good things" (as she sees it) and then dutifully doing them just so. (King Alcinoos and Queen Arete's house or garden or dining room would fit right in to *Martha Stewart Living*, and rightly so.)

The Phaecians want you to be the best you can be, and they want to teach you how.

But they can overdo. The downside to Phaecia has a hard edge. Martha Stewart's helpful, earnest, didactic approach to perfected homemaking can seem to some to be fussy and perfectionistic. Some visitors to the Phaecians find them to be pale and bloodless do-gooders; in the extreme they are caricatures of the virtuous. In that case their perfectionism is heavy and hectoring, rather than graceful and helpful. As Mark Twain said of some likely Phaecian wanna-be, "He was a good man in the worst sense of the word."

We meet Phaecians in organizations and environments focused on rules and regulations that prescribe "the right way" for things to be done. They direct, correct and admonish. This is where you will find lists of Habits of Highly Effective People. There may be explicit dress codes, protocols for doing business, for making sales and interacting with management. They may even prescribe the high-minded attitudes and thoughts with which work ought be done. Right and wrong will be crystal clear; as with Laestrygonia, there is little gray area in Phaecia. For good or for ill, these worlds are adamant that the details be tightly managed.

Such Phaecian companies can thrive when products require mistake-free precision, like the manufacture of pharmaceuticals or sensitive high technology.

But some Phaecian organizations get caught in the trap of compulsively getting the details right, and end up more concerned about enforcing their rigid standard operating procedures, rather than responding to customer needs and to the realities of the marketplace. This is the Total Quality movement gone awry. Zero defects, when unnecessary, can be maddening as well as ineffective. Taken to an extreme, the Phaecian culture may seem to others self-righteous, critical and unforgiving.

The Phaecians bless Odysseus with vast treasures, fine clothing, bronze and gold, far exceeding the spoils of war that he won at Troy and lost on his journey.

Then at long last, the Phaecians and Odysseus set sail for Ithaca, and just as the sun rises they land at Odysseus' island. Odysseus sleeps, so the Phaecian crew lay him gently on the sands of the beach of Ithaca, and nearby they store the rich gifts they have given him.

The desires stirred in the Land of the Lotos Eaters, the steadfast will to escape the Cyclops, the inspiring, crystal clear vision of home from Aeolus, the arduous journey to hell and back, and the promises implicit in Circe's wisdom and Calypso's attentions are fulfilled by the Phaecians, people of the highest virtue who remind you of your own.

**You'll know you're in Phaecia when:**

- The central focus of the community is on virtue, as they see it: on doing the right thing, and teaching others to do and to be their best.
- Quality is the by-word. But sometimes the quest for perfection makes Phaecians rigid and judgmental.
- The locals strive to be orderly and honorable. There is a right way to do things, and one *should* discern and do the right thing.

**If you are in Phaecia:**

- Decisionmaking is principled. What is our duty? Phaecians seek to do good, and they are willing to let the chips fall where they may. Don't argue for the quick and dirty fix.

- Respect authority in this place. Follow the chain of command. Go through channels. Honor tradition. Respect the elders. Odysseus knows that the proper procedures are to ask Queen Arete on his knees for passage home, and he does so.
- Show your virtues. This is not the place to hide your light under a bushel. Without exercising your virtues you can't make it home.
- Play the game. Phaecians want everyone to participate.
- Tell your story so that you can be seen for the unique hero that you are.

# PART THREE

CHAPTER TWELVE

# Home Again

*"Home.........."*
— E.T.

*"There's no place like home. There's no place like home."*
— DOROTHY GALE, *THE WIZARD OF OZ* (L. FRANK BAUM)

Now Odysseus is back on Ithaca after 20 long, tempestuous years. Athene creates a secret identity for her superhero as a decrepit beggar, so as not to raise suspicions. He makes his way back to his real life and his real estate, and, now that he is home, the place of reckoning, he is recognized for himself in dizzying succession:

1. Odysseus privately reveals himself to his son Telemachus for the great man that he truly is, which when you think of it, is a wondrous and uncommon thing for a father to

do. (How many fathers hide their true virtues from their sons, pretending to be something less?)

2. His beloved, old dog Argos (over 20 years old, 140 in dog years!) knows him right away.
3. He makes himself known to his loyal swineherd Eumaeus and his cowherd Philoitos, and they agree to fight the suitors who haunt Penelope.
4. His nurse Eurycleia recognizes him when she washes the familiar, old scar on his thigh.
5. And then, at Odysseus' house, the 108 greedy and profligate suitors who have been stalking Penelope all these years make the fatal recognition that the sad sack *shlepper* in their midst is none other than the great Odysseus come home.

And so you have it. How do we recognize someone for who he truly is? We are best recognized for who we *really* are (1) by our issue — our children and our creations, (2) by those beings who love us, (3) by our trustworthy allies, (4) by those old wounds we bear, truly and deeply, and perhaps most of all, alas, (5) by the enemies we've made, and the way, heroic or otherwise, that we engage them.

Odysseus is heroic indeed: In a much celebrated, impressively gory battle, father and son and the two loyal herdsmen massacre the lot of gentlemen callers. The team wreaks terrible carnage, and with their triumph Odysseus reclaims his house and kingdom.

## Don't Sit Under the Olive Tree With Anyone Else But Me

With each recognition Odysseus has recollected a part of himself. But there is one recognition left undone, and it is by far the most profound and central for a homecoming of the soul. No one can see Odysseus as clearly as his dear wife and soul mate Penelope, and there is no one to whom he can so plainly show himself.

With the suitors slain, Penelope enters the great hall and sits opposite the great man, her husband.

After 20 years of aggravation, frustration and dashed hopes, this could be an hysterical, ungrounded, overwrought moment. But here we have two cool customers; both are masterfully self-possessed, and they are well-matched.

They do not hurry into each others' arms as in a slow-motion TV commercial for a hair product. On the contrary, the text tells us his eyes look down and away; immensely patient, he waits for his wife to speak, but she sits in restrained silence.

Consider the event: here are grand lovers who meet after many years. Their passionate pull to each other is palpable in the room, but they both hold back. Why? Sometimes when there is the most to say, so little can be said. They do not dissipate the moment with chatter.

For their son Telemachus, his mother's self-possession is unbearable.

*Mother, why do you keep away from my father in this way?*
*Why do you not sit by his side and talk to*
*him and ask him questions?*
*No other woman could bear to keep away from her*
*husband when he had come back to her after twenty years*
*of absence, and after having gone through so much!*[34]

She replies, "If he is truly Odysseus, we have secret tokens between us that only we know. We will recognize each other for certain."

Penelope unquestionably *knows* who he is. His life's energy is unmistakable. But she will demand something more of him. She wants to know if he remembers how utterly profound their relationship is.

Penelope delays because she has a plan, a tease, a delicious, sly test.

She calls out to the nurse. "Eurycleia, make up the bed from the master bedroom with covers and blankets. And then *move it* to the hallway."

But Odysseus knows, and Penelope, and only a single servant, that long ago when he built their magnificent marriage bed, Odysseus made one bedpost out of a living olive tree and then erected their bedroom around this most embedded of all beds, and then their house around the bedroom. Their secret is that their marriage bed, like their relationship, is grounded and steadfast. It is rooted in the earth. It cannot be moved.

He hears Penelope's orders to the nurse and he is furious. "WHAT?" explodes Odysseus, "*Who cut off my bed?*"

No one could move the bed! Except — is their relationship no longer so deep-rooted as he left it? Her test of *him* is the prospect of *her* infidelity.

How will he react?

Odysseus passes the test: he blows his stack.

Odysseus' ferocity reveals to Penelope's womanly delight that he shares their unique secret: how deep they go, how well-made and secure their relationship is. An imposter would not know the secrets of their "family tree."

Odysseus' intimate knowing is proof certain of his identity. Penelope acknowledges Odysseus at last.

"Don't be cross with me, my darling Odysseus" she says, as she bursts into tears and falls into his arms.

Finally, the great man and his loyal and loving wife Penelope canoodle together, alone at last under their comforters. The text tells us she *locks* her arms bewitchingly around his neck and won't let go; they talk softly to each other, sharing the news from their long time apart, taking turns back and forth. Penelope tells of how she has waited for him and her anguish with the suitors, their profligacy with the sheep and cattle, and their drunken guzzling of the wine.

Odysseus recounts the whole of his adventures and she is rapt; he muses poignantly, compassionately, and with sophistication, about the trouble he caused people on his journey, and the people who had anguished him.

They listen lovingly to each other's stories. What more could you ask? How could they be more themselves than at this moment?

## CHAPTER THIRTEEN

# The Symbolic Life

*Man's ultimate concern must be expressed symbolically, because symbolic language alone is able to express the ultimate.*
— Paul Tillich

*The decisive question for man is 'Is he related to something infinite or not?'*
— C.G. Jung

*Hello, I must be going.*
— Groucho Marx

Odysseus tells Penelope that he has one more adventure yet, and he reveals the instructions that he heard from the soul of Tiresias in Hades: he must carry his oar so far inland to a race of people who know nothing of the ways of sea, until he meets a stranger who will ask about the oar, "Is that a fan to winnow grain?"

(A winnowing fan blows air to separate the grain from the chaff; it divides and sorts, a process called threshing. Winnowing operates much like conventional thinking: it separates wholes into their component parts, makes distinctions, analyzes, chooses and categorizes. It seeks to explain and understand.)

"No," Odysseus must tell him. Perhaps he continues, "It's not a tool for threshing. It is exactly the opposite. It is something called a *symbol.*"

A *symbol* (*sym*: together, *ballein*: throw) facilitates communication between humans and the gods. It brings them together, mediating between their worlds, keeping them connected. A symbol can be anything — a word, an image, an object — that *makes it personal* between man and god. (Or in the words of a famous latter day leader, perhaps, the symbol is "a uniter, not a divider.")

A symbol is precisely the contrary of threshing: it does not seek to explain or dissect or understand, but to communicate the whole with an integral insight.

By taking his oar — the symbol of his journey — inland, Odysseus spreads the news of the dominions of the gods on earth, and how they work in concert with humankind, to people who have not yet come to terms with the gods.

His reward, promised by Tiresias, is discharge of his obligations to Poseidon, and then a long and happy life on earth and a peaceful death.[35]

Odysseus is off Poseidon's barbed fishhook at long last, and you can be sure that if this were not just the deal that touchy and demanding Poseidon wants for himself, he would not let Odysseus out from under.

It's a good deal all around, but why? What's in it for Poseidon?

The god's motives remain a mystery, a consternation, as they must; but Poseidon's long-standing discontent is cured by this new joint venture with Odysseus to tell their mutual story; and it can only be that Poseidon too wants to be known for who he is, and more at-home in the world as well. Gods need to be believed in.

With the sacrifice ("making sacred") of his oar, Odysseus changes the essential meaning of his journey from a difficult trip where his ego was sometimes battered and sometimes exalted (an ego trip) into something divine, *a gift for the gods*, and as a consequence, an inspiration for all who touch his story.

Odysseus surpasses himself: he enters what Jung called "The Symbolic Life"; he is awake to the consequence of his life. "When people feel that they are living the symbolic life, that they are actors in the divine drama," Jung wrote, "that gives the only meaning to human life; everything else is banal and you can dismiss it. A career, producing of children, all are maya compared with that one thing, that your life is meaningful."[36]

Odysseus has been caught up in the divine drama for a while now; you might say that he and Poseidon have been travel partners of a kind. But with the sacrifice of the oar in a far place where Poseidon is unknown, the relationship *transforms.* Odysseus is no longer a *victim* of the divine, he is a *collaborator.* This intimate collaboration with the gods is the decisive consequence of Odysseus' long journey, and it is what the gods want and need to exercise their dominion. That is why the covenant is a good deal all around.

Ultimately, Odysseus changes the universe by first changing his view of himself. Instead of being a victim of a vengeful, implacable god, he collaborates in a sacred universe in which he is essential.

Truth be told, the universe was always sacred, always pregnant with the possibility of the collaboration of gods and humans, but now he *knows* that he *is* an integral part: the immortals cannot be fully who they are without him, nor he without them.

*how would man exist*
*how would you exist*
*if God did not need him*
*did not need you?*
— BUBER

Where is this far inland place where the gods are not known, and where the natives are so misguided as to mistake a magical oar for a farm implement?

The German social philosopher Max Weber lamented the over-rational and over-intellectual approach of the modern world, the dogma that logical thinking, science and objectivity would not only *explain* the world we live in, but would give us the tools to *master the universe*. Weber said the industrial, technological, impersonal society — materialistic and machine-like — led to what he famously called "the disenchantment of the world," the displacement of the gods and magic, which is to say the Mystery of life, from our lives.

The place where Poseidon is not known is the very world that we live in, the place in each of us where the Mystery has been forgotten. When Odysseus brings his story of the astonishing sea god to where the god is not known, he re-enchants the world.

(This is how Socrates[37] and the early critics of Homer missed his point: they were trying to clear up the mysteries, to make ethical and logical sense, to shine the light of proper thinking on a world in which too much is chaotic and hard to fathom. But

Homer's method is the opposite; he intends to re-enchant the world, to invite more of the Mystery back in.)

And so the unspoken intent of *The Odyssey* is not to get home after all, not to be your true self, however wonderful and rich that part of the journey surely is. How empty it would be if the trip were just for Odysseus' own salvation.

The *meaning* of this odyssey emanates from a *relationship* that needs therapy: from the need to heal the rift between gods and men. Man's part is to invite the gods to be at-home in the world too, in places where they are not known, whether that be a faraway place or our own heart.

Wouldn't it be nice if we all had clear instructions from the spirit of the clairvoyant Tiresias, later confirmed by the enchantress Circe, about how to get Poseidon off our backs?

But of course we do. The instructions are fairly simple: First, Tiresias says, be wary of the Cattle of the Sun, those shiny, seductive, worldly false idols. Then, with the direction to sacrifice your story to the gods, he says: *out of the muck of your experiences, you must re-enchant the world.* One sees this transparently among those who have been redeemed from addiction, injury, illness, a criminal past, or hard times, and who then go on to bring magic to those who still suffer their travails.

> *"The wand chooses the wizard, Mr. Potter."*
> — MR. OLLIVANDER, PROPRIETOR OF THE MAGIC WAND SHOP, TO HARRY POTTER

But we all have had our travels, and each of us has a corner of the world that is ours to re-enchant. "Each man has a sphere of being, far extended in place and time," writes Martin Buber, "which is allotted to him to be redeemed through him."[38] It is unlikely to be some Great Secret; most people, if pressed to say, know very well what portion of the world they are charged with redeeming and what of their experiences and skills they are to bring to the task.

It is the part of the journey that bedevils our own lives. It is the part of this odyssey where we find ourselves *right now.* How do you heal this strange place, so that it will loose its grip and let you move on?

Each true-told story is like Odysseus' oar: it redeems other travelers, it lets the gods be seen for themselves, it is a symbol that makes the connection between the world of soul and the world of people.

And, now his oar sacrificed to the gods, the journey of Odysseus ends where it began, where he is at-home in Ithaca, and king and husband and father. He lives to old age beloved by Athene and at peace with Poseidon, a collaborator with the gods on earth, and with a good story to tell.

*"The story is not ended. It has not yet become history,*
*and the secret life it holds can break out tomorrow*
*in you or in me."*
— Gershon Scholem

*Always keep Ithaca in your mind.*
*To arrive there is your ultimate goal.*
*But do not hurry the voyage at all.*
*It is better to let it last for many years;*
*and to anchor at the island when you are old,*
*rich with all you have gained on the way.*
— Constantine P. Cavafy (1911)

# PART FOUR

APPENDIX ONE

# A Travelin' Man

*"I'm a travelin' man."*
— Ricky Nelson

*"What was* The Odyssey, *after all, but a road movie?"*
— Roger Ebert

*"My purpose in making this wonderful journey is not to delude myself but to discover myself in the objects I see."*
— Goethe, *Italian Journey*

Odysseus is a travelin' man, if ever there was one. He lurches from one fantastical land to another, one set of premises to another. He is nothing if not flexible and resilient. Oh, he struggles, he grizzures, he gets impossibly lost. But then, like Kerouac or Willie Nelson, he is on the road again.

But Odysseus is definitely not someone you could call a tourist (one who "tours," a sightseer). Tourists like to take close charge of their trips; usually they want to follow a tight itinerary so that they can maximize their time and money, and minimize uncertainty and the local muss and fuss.

Tourists will want to bring along what they can of the comforts of home to insulate themselves against the exigencies of chance. But what a tourist most of all carries with him, to keep himself *really* comfortable, is a mindset, a certain way of looking at the world and a set of opinions about how to operate. By necessity, a tourist stays in his cocoon "on the outside looking in" of wherever he visits.

That's not Odysseus. He is instead the quintessential *traveler* (O.F., "one who suffers travails"). (Indeed, the name Odysseus is usually translated as "man of pain;" the Coen brothers in their wonderful film *O Brother, Where Art Thou?*, dubbed their bluegrass version of Odysseus "a man of constant sorrow.")

A traveler *participates* in the life of the places where he finds himself. He's not just passing through. Traveling, by definition, means being present and engaged; it means being attentive and vulnerable to the beings you meet and to the drama you are in. The traveler necessarily emerges changed from his relationships and from his experiences. For the traveler, it's personal.

But, because he must be open to people and events, the traveler is much less in control of his experience than a tourist, and much less inoculated. The traveler Paul Theroux writes, "The essence of travel is discomfort and discovery."

A tourist guide covers the principal sights, where to eat and sleep, the way to change real money into the local scrip, and how to deal with the native customs. In a good tourist book, everything useful should be right there on the page, not open to ambiguity.

But the *Odyssey* is no tourist book. It is a guide for travelers: it is about how to *travel*, how to *engage your own journey* which has a life of its own. It is this *participating consciousness* that is at the very heart of *The Odyssey*.

*Proclus was indeed right*: *The Odyssey* teaches not mastery but a *perspective* — a way of traveling through experience so as to find your way home.

As you journey with Odysseus, you too can bring along the rock-solid truths you are certain of, the values you don't have to think about, the person you know for sure to be who you truly are. You can be a tourist.

These beliefs and perspectives that you *schlep* along are the comforts of home that a tourist carries with him. They are like my goose down pillow that I like to carry on my trips when I can, that holds my head in the same place that it is at home.

Or you can be with Odysseus, a fellow traveler. He is open to discovery and to contingency and to being affected. He knows that he must pay close attention to where he is, because as he travels, the customs and premises will shift. He must take the beings he meets seriously, as the success of the journey depends on his encounters with them.

A traveler brings himself along on the journey, not just his pillow.

So the truth of *The Odyssey,* because it's a book for travelers and not a tourist guide, won't be found on the page at all, although many search hard there, with a good dictionary of the Greek in one hand, and a magnifying glass in the other. They hope to figure the true meaning by rational and scientific investigation, probing for the literal truth in the Homeric texts by Talmudically parsing the Greek, by counting the syllables and deconstructing the meter. They are like those who try to fathom insight by studying the anatomy of the eye.

Philosopher Ken Wilber writes, "If you want to study *Macbeth* empirically, you can get a copy of the play and subject it to various scientific tests; it weighs so many grams, it has so many molecules of ink, it has this number of pages...But if you want to know the meaning of the play, you will have to read it and enter into its interiority, its meaning, its intentions, its depths."[39]

*"Overdraw me Lord, and who cares if I break."*
— KAZANTZAKIS

*The Odyssey,* like any journey, is a mystery whose meaning comes from the actual traveling of it. Nobody can tell before he hits the road what will turn out to be significant for him, where he will find that moment of refraction, and what will roll off his back. It is only by traveling that each traveler discovers what his powers — his virtues — are; it is only through his adventures that the traveler experiences himself as an individual, unique, creative in his way, and blind in his way.

The travails of the traveler reveal the traveler to himself.

APPENDIX TWO

# The Man of Many Turns

Achilles was handsome and fair-haired, the principal hero of the Greeks in *The Iliad*. He was the most magnificent warrior of his day, but everyone knew he had a whopping temper; his anger and resentment raged out of control.

Like some proud street tough who is especially sensitive to being *dissed*, Achilles feels obliged to take crushing revenge on those who mess with him. For his lack of pity, Achilles was something of a heel.

In his ruinous dispute with his fellow general Agamemnon over the distribution of concubines, he puts the entire Greek army at risk when he petulantly refuses to fight. Later, after he kills the Trojan Prince Hector to avenge the death of his best pal Patroclus, he is still so enraged that he needlessly humiliates the Trojans by dragging Hector's corpse behind his chariot.

Achilles is blinded by his own rage. He can't get outside his tumultuous pride and resentment to see a larger picture, let alone to sensibly evaluate what's really happening. He has no context, so he goes overboard. Much like the Cyclops Polyphemus who has just one eye, Achilles has just the *one way of looking* at events, and that is from his own egocentric point of view.

Although they were comrades-in-arms at Troy, Odysseus and Achilles are worlds apart. Odysseus, too, is recognized in his own time as a great warrior and also as a wise counselor, a persuasive speaker, and a true leader. But where Achilles made the case to take Troy head-on, by crushing force, Odysseus concocted the clever Trojan Horse stratagem which won the day.

Odysseus is no masterful, overpowering movie action hero. He is no Achilles, and he is no John Wayne, who, with big guns and a droll put-down slays the desperados and looks good and feels righteous doing it.

The true experience of traveling with Odysseus is always a defeat for this kind of gun-slinging *mastery*. In nearly every instance Odysseus or his men are beaten or eaten or shipwrecked or stoned. He reels and lurches. At times he is awash in self-pity or immobilized by his own foolishness. He endures long delays and false starts, and he makes big, big mistakes. He loses control of his troops at critical moments. One could not honestly say that he is master of his fate except in his reliable and uncanny penchant for getting knocked around.

A clue from the story: While Odysseus emerges a great man and a great hero from his difficult journey, in *The Odyssey* he conquers no one except, most instructively, the interlopers in his own house.

He bobbles the ball again and again, one mistake after another. Yet, at each stop along the way, something startling: he makes the trip his own and no one can deny it. But how does he do it?

Odysseus' most celebrated and characteristic epithet comes from the first line of *The Odyssey*: Homer says that he is *anthropos polytropos*, "the man of many turns" (Gr. *tropos*, turn, way, manner, style). He has many "tropes," *many ways of looking* at things. He is *versatile* (Lt. turns easily), ingeniously adjusting his perspective to changing circumstances. Unlike Achilles or most heroes of his day or since, Odysseus is not locked into a singular mindset that he tries to impose on the rest of the world.

Odysseus' critics in classical Greece, even the great Socrates himself, who called Homer's work "ugly lies,"[40] misconstrued this quality: they thought that Odysseus changed his basic nature too easily, that he was a slippery chameleon, that he had no character. Odysseus was viciously caricatured by the playwright Sophocles as a slick, self-interested confidence man who tries to trick the innocent, hard luck archer Philoctetes[41] to fight at Troy. And by the time of Pericles at the height of Athenian power and culture in the fifth century BCE, writes the classicist William Stanford, if "the whole body of well-informed Athenians had been asked to vote for [Odysseus'] condemnation or acquittal on the question of his moral worth, they would probably have condemned him."[42]

Times have changed. Socrates, falsely convicted of heresy and of corrupting the minds of the young, chose the death penalty when he could have chosen exile; to the consternation of many, he insisted upon his own death as a matter of principle. It has always been easy enough to find principles to die for, if you are so inclined. But it is the project of living that is far more problematic. And our hero Odysseus is all about the project of living, which, said another way, is the journey to find home.

Odysseus' critics did not understand his character because they did not understand the nature of the journey he is obliged to take. On the journey home, even the most basic assumptions — about what is significant and valuable, about how to treat the natives, about what will get you stuck and what will get you back on the road — must be fluid and responsive to the facts on the ground.

We learn with Odysseus a crucial fact: that what works well for him in one place may not work in another. The sweet talk at Calypso's has little currency with a Cyclops. Lists of highly effective habits for self-improvement won't help you much on this odyssey (except at the Phaecians', who go in for that sort of thing). On a journey such as this you can't be fighting the last battle or the next one. You can't get stuck in a leftover mindset from a long gone adventure if you want to get home.

Each alien land that Odysseus visits holds particular assumptions about how the world works. The paranoid, high-strung Laestrygonians are centrally worried that travelers are out to get them, and that they must defend themselves against their visitors with devastating pre-emptive strikes. The high-minded Phaecians believe it is most important to do their honorable duty in all circumstances, with perhaps reckless disregard of the consequences to themselves. The laid-back Lotos Eaters emphasize the need to take things easy, to turn on and drop out, and do not worry too much about the arduous journey ahead.

When Odysseus does not travel gracefully or well, when he does not learn the lessons of the land where he is, he gets stuck in a place, *overtaken by its premises*. He gets mired in a mindset; the perspectives of that place hold him hostage.

Most people we meet are stuck in some episode of their Odyssey, without even realizing it. They take on the beliefs and attitudes — the culture or the *personality* — of that place. A personality is a *position,* a set of presumptions, a framework to understand and deal with the events of life. These largely unconscious assumptions, closely held opinions, inclinations and expectations drive the way we see ourselves, value our world, create our relationships and do our work.

Trapped in our story, we generally allow in information that supports our episode's frame of reference. We reject or remake information that will not fit. We interpret other people's behaviors through that perspective, even though they may have a different frame: *they* may be mired with Calypso (feeling sorry for themselves), and *we* are getting down with Aeolus (imagining the wonderful future yet in store.) To independent Circe, clingy Calypso will seem desperately codependent. To the security-conscious Laestrygonians, who think that the whole world is out to get them, the earnest, transparent Phaecians will seem reckless and irresponsible.

Once stuck in a frame of reference, we meet the same frustrations, battle the same monsters and chimeras that return again and again; time after time the same intrusive gods want their due. And all the while, out of ignorance or pride or recalcitrance, we reject the help and blessings of our powerful allies, those wise beings and immortals and fellow travelers who are ready to lend a hand. *Until,* at last, somehow, that strange place comes to terms with us, and lets loose its spell, and we come to terms with it; and we relax our grip and are able to move on.

If we know the place where someone has landed (or is stranded) in *The Odyssey*, we know a lot about them: we know something of their philosophy of life; we know what is significant to them, what their strengths are and what their blind spots are likely to be. We know something of their struggle, and who the locals are that they must deal with, the monsters that haunt them and the divine beings who can help.

You can then be *polytropos* — "of many turns" — yourself. And as Homer says famously of Odysseus, you can "know the minds of many men" and "be skilled in all ways of contending." You can get out of your own way and see the world through the circumstances of others. You need not lug your unwieldy frame of reference along with you to places where it is less elegant or suitable. (Much of the *tsuris* in the world comes because we are bollixed up in some alien land where we frantically try to impose upon the natives the customs that we learned from another place.) You can be engaged with the adventure that shows up, and not the one that you had imagined, or hoped for or dreaded.

This is perhaps not as Socrates would have wished. No objective logic or Socratic method gets Odysseus through or saves him. Each adventure instead has an internal logic; it makes sense on its own terms. No singular attitude or set of beliefs makes Odysseus great. He holds only to the conviction that he must get home to his real life, and that he will do what works. He's not out to prove some grand philosophy of life. If he has a baseline, it is simply that he will not settle for cheap imitations: he won't give up his real soul mate Penelope for the gorgeous but needy goddess Calypso, and he won't give up his real home, even for a spiffy if starchy Utopia on Scheria.

As with Odysseus, each new land can be nourishing as it reveals its significance; but if the traveler is stuck, or if he overstays (as at Calypso's), even paradise can be a prison.

To know where a traveler has settled down, we have only to look at what they value, what they pay attention to, their habits of mind. What is of most significance? How do they pretend the world works?

The easygoing Lotos Eaters create a low-stress, low-conflict environment. They prefer to go with the flow and not to rock the boat; they are mired in routine and complacency. They do not tolerate discomfiting feelings or painful longings, most particularly the ache for home. Instead they prefer to relax, and to accommodate to what they have. Lotos Eaters are disinclined to start out on the journey, and, once they do, are reluctant to change direction and to make decisions. This is the place to overcome inertia, take action and head for home.

The Cyclopes are forces of nature who enjoy their libidinous appetites without restriction, reservation or regret in a rough and tumble universe. Travelers may be repelled by their bullying, excess and lack of propriety and scruples. In this place the traveler, as well as the Cyclops, confronts his relationship to the exercise of his own potency, whether he be ruthless or faint-hearted. This is the place to learn how to act with power and make one's mark in the world.

Aeolus and his family are optimists who see the world as a cornucopia of possibilities and imaginative ideas. They are engaging, high energy and upbeat. But they are inflexibly optimistic: they insist on good vibes and will have nothing to do with the inevitable pitfalls along the road that come with being mortal. They are gifted visionaries, brilliant at imagining the future, but not so brilliant at actually getting there. This is a great place for brainstorming, for making plans, and for picturing and relishing what Ithaca will be like in great detail.

The nervous Laestrygonians want, most of all, to feel safe and secure. Paranoid and hyperalert, they are preoccupied with downside scenarios: they worry about what can go wrong, who will do them in, and who can be trusted (likely no one). They see the world in terms of enemies and allies. ("You are either with us or against us.") Laestrygonia is the place for the traveler to confront his own individual doubts and fears. Here is the opportunity to grow courage and self-affirmation, in spite of the harsh judgments of the Laestrygonians.

Circe is an emotionally detached teacher, advisor and guide. She easily enchants humans, but serves those who know their own mind. Aeaea is the place to reflect upon your journey, to confront your own enchantments and to get valuable guidance from a mentor about the road ahead.

The melancholy shades in Hades, the Land of the Dead, are consumed with remorse over wrong life choices, and what might have been. They cling to failed dreams and a painful past. Hades is the land of "if only," a place we are all destined to visit at one time or another. Those who don't come to terms with their unlived lives, regrets, jealousies, ambitions and cravings are mired here for eternity.

In the straits between Scylla and Charybdis the emphasis is on cool efficiency, on the bottom line, on getting to the goal. In these dire straits you will be judged strictly by your results, by how efficient and effective you are at getting through despite the monstrous obstacles and *inevitable* losses; here no one much cares how deep are your feelings, how noble is your intent, or how profound is your understanding.

Seductive, nourishing, and affirming, the goddess Calypso works hard to make herself indispensable, appreciated and adored. With laser-precise sensitivity to a traveler's needs, feelings, appetites and preferences, she is indeed a brilliant helpmate; but left to her own devices she can be self-serving, manipulative and demanding, as she sinks her hooks into you. As she tries to create dependency, Calypso tests a traveler's independence, dignity and self-worth. With her magical ability to flood a traveler with whatever comforts might be imagined, the traveler must distill which needs are real and which are false.

The idealistic Phaecians are concerned with duty, honor and responsibility, and with doing things the correct way according to the highest standards. They let the chips fall where they may, even to their own detriment. A traveler must tell his story and show his virtues here. If he does, the Phaecians may give him a lift home.

What am I doing here? What really matters now? What do the gods demand? What does this encounter invite? These are the questions a traveler asks. The traveler who fails to ask these questions — to investigate his predicament, to make it conscious — will surely get mired in one of these strange, faraway places, a victim of the local complexes which have a lives and intentions of their own.

The answers to these questions, which is to say the *meaning* of the trip, change with each traveler, and change as each traveler moves on.

APPENDIX THREE

# Allegory

*"Some events happened that are not true.*
*Others are true but did not happen."*
— Elie Weisel

*"If Moby Dick has a part to play in an allegory,*
*he is none the less a whale."*
— George deF. Lord

*"My mummy always said there were no monsters,*
*no real ones — but there are."*
— Agent Ripley, *Alien Resurrection*

*The Odyssey* has long and widely been interpreted as allegory, so that the perspicacious goddess Circe was said by many to be a stand-in for "wisdom" and the high-minded Phaecians represented "the principled life." Plato said that the lotos of the Lotos Eaters amounted to "false and arrogant reasonings and opinions."[43]

Even early commentators assumed that the rapacious gods and goddesses could not be taken *literally.* The first century philosopher Heraclitus commented that "If Homer were not an allegorist, he would be completely impious."[44]

For all the untold discussion about Homer over thousands of years—and every conceivable interpretation has been proffered and disputed—no one (to my knowledge) has been able to seriously argue that he was inarticulate or imprecise. Perhaps Homer said what he meant to say.

I wonder if there is a traveler reading this, someone who has truly been on the road, who has not actually met Calypso, not a figurative Calypso, a painting or a sculpture or an allegory, but the goddess herself: she who has served up just the comforts and pleasures that are needed just when the traveler is desperate for them, and then, in an instant, the traveler has overstayed and can't find a decent way to leave.

Odysseus is not the last traveler to have *within his grasp* a clear-as-crystal vision of life-as-it-could-and-should-be, with the people and the financing nearly in place, such as the brilliant vision of Ithaca that Aeolus gins up for Odysseus, only to see it vanish into thin air, gone with the wind. No, that's far too gruesome for a fairy tale.

And is there anyone who, with nothing but innocent intent, has served on a committee in a professional organization or a charity, who has not met at least one gnarly Laestrygonian who hated him on sight, who wants him out or worse, who doesn't want to talk things through, who bombards him every which way, and for no apparent reason? How *allegorical* are those delusional, paranoid Laestrygonians?

And some people, alas, spend their whole emotional lives in Hades, as much and *as truly as* Agamemnon, Achilles and Ajax do, wistfully moping about, envious of the living, regretful over their own wrong life choices, stewing for revenge at those who hurt them long ago, drowning in the disappointment of what might have been. For people really stuck in Hades, the philological research proving that oral folktales of a journey to the Underworld were common long before Homer just doesn't matter much.

Perhaps most telling of all, I used to think that the 20 years that Odysseus was away, the 10 years at the wars and the 10 years struggling to find his way home was surely an *allegory*; that Homer probably meant to indicate something like "an awfully long time." But now looking back, I know that Homer certainly meant it *at least literally*; and in fact maybe 20 years isn't even long enough to make it home.

## ACKNOWLEDGEMENTS

Some friends graciously read the manuscript. I am much obliged for their interest and insight. Thank you to Kasey Arnold-Ince, Thomas Condon, Walter Effross, Tom Flautt, Ted Grabowski and Kirby Olson. Nancy Jean Amick believed in the mission, even as Odysseus seemed hopelessly mired in the muck.

Special thanks to Michele DeFilippo of 1106 Design for her excellent book design and production wisdom.

## ENDNOTES

1. Robert Lamberton and John J. Keany, eds, *Homer's Ancient Readers,* (Princeton: Princeton University Press, 1992) p20.
2. James Hastings, *Encyclopedia of Religion and Ethics* (Edinburgh: T&T Clark, 1922) Vol 6, p759.
3. Carl G. Jung, *Collected Works* (CW) 7, p174.
4. Jung, CW 7, p269.
5. Søren Kierkegaard, *Either/Or,* Vol. I: Diapsalmata (Penguin Classics, 1992).
6. Homer, *Odyssey* (Samuel Butler) Book IX.
7. *Ibid.*
8. *Ibid.*
9. A gift from Maron, a priest of Apollo.
10. Freud also used the term libido. Of course Freud and Jung famously disagreed over whether the *source* of this driving intention was sexual (Freud) or a broader life energy (Jung).
11. Sigmund Freud, "New Introductory Lectures." *Standard Edition,* Vol. 22. (1933) p73.
12. C.G. Jung, "The Concept of Libido," CW 5, par. 194.
13. Claudio Naranjo, *Ennea-Type Structures* (Nevada City CA; Gateways Publishers, 1990) p127.
14. B. W. Tuckman, Development Sequence in Small Groups" *Psychological Bulletin,* 1965, Vol. 63, No. 6, p384–399.

15. Jeffrey Toobin, *Too Close to Call* (New York: Random House, 2001) p271.
16. *Ibid.*
17. Homer, *The Odyssey,* (Samuel Butler, trans, 1900) Book X.
18. We can also project as shadow positive qualities — our true leadership, our true authority, our easy grace, our virtues — so that they will seem like they come from others, those people we admire or those we are jealous of. Projecting our positive qualities is equally self-invalidating and lacking in self-recognition, of course.
19. Paul Tillich, *The Courage to Be* (New Haven: Yale University Press, 1952) p3.
20. Merriam-Webster, *Merriam-Webster's Collegiate Dictionary & Thesaurus,* Deluxe Audio Edition (Version 3.0); CD-Rom edition (July, 2003).
21. George de Forest Lord, *Homeric Renaissance* (North Haven CT: Archon Books, 1972) p112.
22. Carl Jung, "On the Nature of the Psyche," CW 8, par. 425.
23. Adam Phillips, *On Flirtation* (Cambridge: Harvard University Press, 1996) p151.
24. Homer, *Odyssey* (Butler) Book XIII, re-imagined.
25. Merriam-Webster, *op.cit.*
26. *Ovid's Metamorphosis Englished, Mythologized and Represented in Figures.* 1632. Edited by Karl K. Hulley and Stanley T. Vandersall. (Lincoln: University of Nebraska Press, 1970) p646.
27. C.G. Jung, "Concerning Rebirth" CW 9, Part I: *The Archetypes and the Collective Unconscious.*(1940) p221.
28. James Hillman, *Insearch: Psychology and Religion,* Second Revised Ed., (Woodstock, CT: Spring Publications, 1996) p103.
29. Jung, CW 9 Section 422.
30. Jung limited the anima to the interior feminine of men, but a growing modern literature ascribes the anima to the interior

feminine of both men and women, an idea which seems self-evident. See for example, James Hillman, *Anima: An Anatomy of a Personified Notion* (Dallas: Spring Publications, 1985).

31. In this sense Ogygia and Lotos Land, both pleasure islands, are precise opposites; the Lotos Eaters hold their broad spectrum narcotics in their open hand, snaring any passers-by who may be attracted; solicitous Calypso seduces individual persons of her own choosing, her appeal is targeted and made-to-order.
32. Carl Jung, *The Syzygy CW,* 9ii para 24.
33. Homer, (Butler) *op.cit.* Book VIII.
34. Homer (Butler) *op.cit.* Book XXIII.
35. This surely is not the deal that some heroes get — like Orion, or Perseus or Heracles — who, when they died, were rewarded with their transcendent place in the heavens, as constellations. Odysseus, most interestingly, has the opposite arrangement. By taking the story of the Sea God to people ignorant of him, Odysseus brings the heavens (the transcendent) down to earth. He constellates the Mystery here on earth.
36. Jung, *op.cit.* CW 18, p275 para 630.
37. See Appendix II.
38. Martin Buber, *Hasidism and Modern Man,* (Philadelphia: University of Pennsylvania Press, 1988) p102.
39. Ken Wilber, *Integral Psychology,* (Boston: Shambala, 2000) p160–1.
40. Lamberton, 1989, *op.cit.* p16.
41. Sophocles, *Philoctetes.*
42. W.B. Stanford, *The Ulysses Theme* (Dallas: Spring Publications, 1992) p100.
43. Plato, *Republic,* Section 560c.
44. Cited in A. A. Long, "Stoic Readings of Homer," in Robert Lamberton, *Homer's Ancient Readers, op. cit.,* p45.

This book is published by Circe's Island Press.

To purchase additional copies of this book visit our website at
*http://www.TravelswithOdysseus.com*

For information about, or to contact, Michael Goldberg visit
*http://www.9WaysofWorking.com*